Being Free

GIBSON WINTER

Being Free

*Reflections on
America's Cultural Revolution*

THE MACMILLAN COMPANY
COLLIER-MACMILLAN LTD., LONDON

These reflections are dedicated to

PHELPS WILDER

a man of work, public responsibility and
humanity to whom these words
would have spoken

The Macmillan Company
866 Third Avenue, New York, N.Y. 10022
Collier-Macmillan Canada Ltd., Toronto, Ontario
Library of Congress Catalog Card Number: 77-119123   OCT 19 '71

First Printing

PRINTED IN THE UNITED STATES OF AMERICA

CONTENTS

51594

TURBULENCE IS NO stranger to America, but seldom in our history have protest and hostility reached such a pitch. Moreover, accusations and countercharges are hurled so recklessly that one is hard put to trace the causes, much less fashion modes of resolution, of the problems. Yet understanding of our situation is indispensable to any constructive action. Somehow we have to discern what is new in our situation and evaluate these new possibilities.

Changes in society and culture came thick and fast in recent decades. At a certain point, these changes seemed to move out of control, and it is difficult to explain this escalation. We were the people who had marshaled science and rational organization to establish the first high technology culture. Poverty, disease and environmental pressures seemed to be yielding to this new system. Even outer space had come within reach. We only had to funnel each new age group through the schooling system, and we could man the system on its course of endless expansion. Then nature began giving back signals of impending disaster. Global wars to end war spawned ever-widening circles of violence. Our urban areas exploded in polarized struggles of White and Black, urban decay and suburban sprawl. Our cherished school system revealed itself as educationally ineffective and socially oppressive. Adding to this expanding disorder, our globe bristled with an ever-present menace of nuclear terror. Confronted with the choice between life and death, man seemed bent upon death.

Escalation of technology to an autonomous, self-determining system probably dates from World War II. The Manhattan Project put man at the mercy of his technological genius. Productive effort for the war raised the power of the system to a new order of magnitude. Massive bureaucracies applied rational principles of control to things and people. Industrial and governmental interests interlocked with expanding military systems. Technology began to operate from its own principles of unlimited growth and expanding domination.

Our task is to discover and empower the human agenda in this computerized world of massive systems. Where is the line which divides healthy growth from destructive exploitation? By what norms do we tame this powerful system? This is the human agenda, and it is already at work within the systems of high technology. Challenges to the system disclose new human possibilities at work against the exploitative powers of high technology. The natural environment has begun to reject the excessive growth of the leviathan. Humanizing forces are at work in national and global struggles for cultural values and identity. The thread which guides us through this maze of conflicting forces is the struggle for liberation. We seem to have reached a new stage in man's agelong quest for a liberated humanity.

Liberation is inextricably bound up with high technology. Our massive populations cannot survive without mass-production systems. Our enlarged humanity depends upon media and complex systems of transportation to realize its possibilities. Thus, groups who would destroy these systems in their search for liberation only court disaster. Technical rationality is not demonic in itself; indeed it is one of man's highest achievements. But its creative power has to be domesticated—it has become a destructive principle.

Our concrete reflections on the struggle for liberation move in a spiral. At first it appears that man can be free when all men share in the goods and capacities of the productive society. However, it becomes apparent that belonging to the system is a necessary but not sufficient condition of liberation. To belong without having a voice is to fall into bondage. Then we come to the further paradox of a revolt by the new generation who share in the affluent society and could easily gain a voice. This leads to the reflection on protest against the productive style of life. Liberation is disclosed as the process of becoming a whole person who can rejoice in nature, respond to beauty, share in poetic visions and participate in intimate human communities. And this search for a human style comes none too soon on the American scene, since automation may very soon make the productive style a secondary activity for most Americans.

At this stage our reflections turn to the most troublesome problem of our day. Technical rationality can only be tamed when we can subordinate the system to a higher principle. But our resources to comprehend such a principle—our democratic and confessional heritages—have been coopted by the system. Democracy has become defined as the American way of life. Denominational faiths have committed their resources to justification of the American system. This is a collapse of transcendence, and many now question whether America can realize its promise as a free people. This is what makes the crisis of technological order a crisis of American culture. Liberation means recovery of those rights of man founded in nature and nature's God. America is now emerging as one limited expression of democracy which is interdependent with many peoples, cultures and faiths who have to have the liberty and space to find their own mode of expression. All peoples participate in the enlarged humanity now being revealed as our common reality, but the liberation of peoples means they must have the power to express their own identities in a pluralistic world. High technology is then disclosed as servant of this liberated humanity—allocating resources and limiting growth on behalf of a participating, pluralistic world.

Our politics have to be utterly realistic in an era of cultural revolution. We easily underestimate the exploitative power of high technology systems. Having become autonomous, these systems impose their images of reality and human fulfillment upon peoples throughout the world. They create a consumer public to which to market their products. They exploit the land and the seas. They coopt the opposition or suppress it. So the citizen in the new age has to test the spirits of technology against his own experience and relationships. We have to demythologize the promises of high technology. We have to seek the truth, cherishing what liberates and sustains life. Often, disciplined abstention is itself liberating. The "gross national product" now has to be written in lower case letters. But this points beyond the present text to the politics of liberation and the style of life for the man and woman of the new age.

A number of authors are cited in a bibliography. These

reflections also depend upon the writings of countless others whose articles and monographs have opened new horizons. Three men have especially helped the author in this text, though unknowingly. Charles Long, a colleague of many years, helped in conversations and articles, pressing the author beyond sociological analysis to fundamental levels of thought. Bernard Meland has always inspired his colleagues with his quiet, penetrating wisdom, and his concept of "enlarged humanity" broke important new ground for the author. Martin Heidegger thinks and writes in concepts somewhat alien to our American mind but fundamental to all human experience. This text owes as immense debt to his thought.

Appreciation is owed to the Detroit Industrial Mission for publishing the original thoughts for this volume as an occasional paper, "Man and Freedom in a Technological Society." The Metropolitan Lectureship of Universities in the Dallas Area, the Urban Training Center in Chicago and the Moravian Seminary furnished opportunities for developing these reflections. Special appreciation is due to Cynthia Donnelly for skillful editing of the manuscript and to Polly Barrows and Rehova Arthur for help with the text.

Gibson Winter
September 15, 1969
Dorset, Vermont

CHAPTER I

The Participatory Society

THROUGH NEWS JOURNALISM and television we are now participants in significant public events. We expect to participate; in fact, we feel that we have a right to share in these events. This is the crucial significance of Marshall McLuhan's insight into the emerging social reality. He contrasts the participatory quality of the new media —profiles of visual and audible communication which evoke involvement—and the more static, individualized experience of linear, written communication. His three stages of communication—oral-interpersonal of the primitive society, linear and written of the higher civilization, and visual-audible of the technological era—help us to

identify the new in our emerging society. He sees the
participatory dimension of electronic communication as
creating a new wholeness of life, a development somewhat
analogous to a worldwide primitivism, in which the isolation and estrangement of the period of nation-states could
be thought of as giving way to an emerging world community of participatory involvement.

This significant insight has been somewhat abused by
excessive publicity in the very media which it attempts to
illumine. We shall have reason to qualify it, but our debt
to Marshall McLuhan is considerable. He has pointed out
the theme of participation which runs through every facet
of our contemporary experience. Our styles of speech,
clothing, thought and morals are being integrated not
only on a national level but globally. Electronic media are
not the only factor in this global integration, but they are
an extremely important element.

A peculiar estrangement occurs simultaneously with
this new participation. This is a paradox of the participatory consciousness which is overlooked in discussions of
the media. We call this a peculiar estrangement because
it reflects the attitude and mind of those who feel they
belong yet know they are excluded. At the very moment
when new possibilities of participatory life open out before our nation and globe, deeper separations estrange us.

The peculiar conjunction of participation and separation is most dramatically apparent in the Black Movement. There are, of course, many Black Movements. The
Black community is no more homogeneous than its White
counterpart. Nevertheless, a Rights Movement did emerge
gradually among Black people following the Supreme
Court decision of 1954 against segregation of schools.
From the Montgomery Bus Boycott to Meredith's March
in Mississippi a restless drive to participate swept
through the Black community—pressuring schools, opening restaurants and motels, breaking color bars in swim-

ming pools and at the polls, crossing discriminatory lines on jobs and even exploding some of the housing covenants. But almost at once the Movement was polarizing from within over the issue of participation or separation. From the Meredith March on, that polarization has intensified. Proponents of participation in the great society are castigated as Uncle Toms by the Black Nationalists. Separatists are disparaged as romantic "Afros" by those who see the only future for the Black American in a unified American society.

We are not making moral judgments on these polarities, only identifying the deep contradiction between the drive to participate and the sense of estrangement, an ambivalence which seems to characterize leaders of the Black Movement as well as segments of the Black community. James Forman demands reparations from the Churches on behalf of the Black people who were exploited under slavery, yet opens the demand with a preamble of violent separatism (See Appendix 1). Even as he is pressing for economic resources to enhance participation in the great society, he is castigating that society and professing separatism. The same is true in different ways of Operation Breadbasket, which merges Black Capitalism with separatist Black Power, as do CORE, SNCC and at least in certain respects even SCLC. There is no way to live within the Black struggle today without straddling these contradictory drives to participation and separation.

The paradox of participation and estrangement is present throughout American society, although it finds dramatic expression in highly visible movements like the Black struggle and student protests. The participatory element was written into the charter of Students for a Democratic Society and has continued to be a major factor in their activities (See Appendix 2). They speak of "participatory democracy" and operate at times in this

fashion, although their 1969 Convention in Chicago shattered over the attempt to allow full participation for a
dissident wing. The press for participation in SDS, however, has to be understood somewhat in the fashion of the
Black struggle. SDS accuses the establishment of denying
participation to youth, Blacks and indeed all impoverished and exploited peoples, including women, Indians,
the Third World and others. In this sense, SDS spear-
heads a drive for participation. It is challenging the exclusion of the masses by an industrial-military clique who
control the great society. However, SDS is also opposed to
this whole establishment and what it has wrought. SDS is
a separatist movement within the great society. Consequently, confrontations over participation are peculiarly
interlaced with a rejection of participation in the great
society. This is the ambivalence which has confounded
university administrators in dealing with SDS-controlled
protests. Every demand for fuller participation is deliv-
ered in such a way and on such terms that it cannot be
negotiated. And it is the nature of this movement that it is
torn between the drive to participate and the compulsion
to separate.

The paradox of a participatory and separated consciousness is dramatically expressed on a world scale.
When Servan-Schreiber published *The Challenge of
America* in France, he could not have dreamed that he
was producing a best seller. At the height of France's
estrangement from America, he proposed that American
organization would dominate Europe unless the Continent
took up the challenge and outdid America. Hostility
against so-called Americanization is yoked with a drive to
participate in the productive society. In Latin America
one encounters a similar ambivalence. The governments
which are polite and the students who protest share a
common drive to enter into the new age of productivity.
They want to participate in the great society. On the

other hand, both leaders and students resent and reject assimilation to this dominating new social reality. The ambivalence is there. The participatory consciousness is an ineradicable element in our new reality. The alienated, estranged, separatist consciousness seems to be an equally powerful factor.

More subtle but more telling indicators of basic trends in social life than collective movements are cultural styles. If we are dealing with a fundamental paradox of contemporary life, we should expect to encounter this paradox of participation and separation in our current styles of art, music, dress and manner. Marshall Mc-Luhan has pretty well demonstrated the crucial place of participatory elements in dress styles, architectural innovation, painting and popular arts. The peculiar phenomenon in this participatory mode is the strangeness, otherness, distance, even inhumanness, of much that now attracts in popular art. The music enchants and engages with its rhythms, but its timbre and mind-blowing character also repel. A similar quality inheres in much contemporary painting—opening primordial participations in a world to which we are still foreign.

Cultural style, notoriously difficult to interpret, is open to many perspectives and insights. One paradoxical theme is the participatory and alienative strain. Nude Theater and Living Theater can perhaps be understood a bit more adequately in terms of this paradox. Both forms are breaking through the objectivity and impersonality of contemporary life—trying to evoke and sustain a more participatory experience. However, both forms reflect the deep poignancy of the isolation and estrangement of man. And strangely enough, both modes of theater deepen the estrangement of the actors and the audience from the participation which they seek to enact and evoke. When a theater critic is carried away by the participatory mode and undresses in the theater, it is above all the actors who are unnerved by his participation. The nakedness of the presentation is itself an expression of the estrangement which the theater seeks to overcome.

On a somewhat less subjective level one senses a similar conjunction of participation and estrangement in the current preoccupation with sensitivity training. The various schools and institutes which are engaging in reeducation to feeling, touch, sensitivity, are trying to break through the alienation and estrangement of contemporary life. They are dealing with estrangement from one another, but also with alienation from feelings, body and sensibilities. The drive to participation is all too evident in this contemporary trend in manners and morals. However, there is also a compulsive quality to this clamor for participation in one another's moods, feelings and organic responses, and at the heart of this compulsion lies a profound, poignant estrangement. In a peculiar way, what is meant as therapy of sensitivity heightens distances and estrangement, because the drive to break through the barriers of contemporary society only makes the actual barriers more threatening and alienating; one heightens estrangement with intense experiences of participation.

The ambivalence in the Black struggle, the student movement, the mind of developing nations and contemporary cultural styles reflects a divided consciousness in our emerging world. We are deeply estranged not only from one another but from that new social reality which is emerging. We appear to be moving further apart even as we experience a new belonging. We feel we are part of it and are aware of our exclusion from it. We accept it and reject it. We belong to it and yet deny it. This is the paradox of our participatory society. The drive to enter into it is accompanied by a compulsion to separate further. Our suburbanization is a parable of this growing estrangement amidst increasing communication, where each new development extends the chain of communication yet builds another isolated enclave. We shall argue, then, that the divided consciousness of participation and estrangement is characteristic of our new world.

THE WEB OF INTERDEPENDENCE

THE PARTICIPATORY CONSCIOUSNESS is grounded in a material web of interdependence. This material base of the media is overlooked when we attribute to electronic communication independent, causal force in shaping our new social reality. Telecommunication is only one facet of a technologically ordered world. Television is the creature of that new technology, and though as a mode of communication it becomes critically important in extending the range and control of the master system, we must try to avoid simplistic explanations of our new world as something special because it has electronic communication. Our new world communicates by mass media because it is a technologically ordered world in which applications of scientific understanding are systematically organized for the execution of human aims. The media are integral to this process. They do not create it any more than they independently shape its new consciousness.

The material web of interdependence creates the conditions for participation even as it provokes the sense of estrangement. We need to understand this new interdependence and the contradictions which it generates. From this perspective, we can look more deeply into the paradox of participation and estrangement which we have begun to identify.

The East Coast of the United States had a dramatic experience of this interdependence during the blackout of 1965. An electric power failure paralyzed many sections of the East Coast for hours—stopping elevators, halting subways and bringing the smoothly organized world of technology to a sudden halt. The shock of the blackout was the awareness of our utter dependence upon a network of functions and services which form an invisible web below the surface of our new world. This material web comes to consciousness only in such crises as the blackout, the Chicago blizzard of 1967 and the New York transit strike. We suddenly realize how tightly wired our system is. We also realize how much of it is below the surface. The new society is like a gigantic iceberg—its infrastructure is an intricate network undergirding our lives.

We call this a web of interdependence because the functions and services make us dependent upon the organization which maintains the network, binding us to one another and to the whole society for our very survival. Strikes in public transportation, slowdowns in air traffic control or strikes by garbage workers make this dependence upon one another's services visible. Most of the time the web operates invisibly, weaving ever-new activities and needs into the fabric of the new society. Our "Spaceship Earth," as Kenneth Boulding has graphically expressed it, is becoming as highly interdependent in functions and control as the Apollo capsules which brought about the touchdown on the moon.

The web of interdependence—our participation in one another and in the larger society through particular functions and exchanges—finds expression in the media. This is how we would interpret the development of participatory consciousness through electronic communication. The participatory consciousness rests upon a material base of dependence and participation. That material web is brought to consciousness and extended by the media.

Newscasts and special televised news events are the rituals of this new participatory society. Day by day, events are rehearsed by newscasters who take their audiences here and there throughout the world by means of personal reports of staff. Most news is actually old hat. It was picked up by the public on the radio or glimpsed in the newspaper. But it has to be reenacted for the participatory power of shaping the consciousness to the events —shaping our world, our time and our social reality. The newscasters are very much like priests of the society, reciting the hours and guaranteeing the continuity of the world. Then when critical events occur—the assassination of a leader, a moon-landing, a papal visit—the event is ritualized again and again for days until all have been drawn into the web and this event becomes their own history.

The material web is not nearly so tightly woven over the globe as within our domestic life, though there are no limits to the range of interdependence which technology can embrace. Telstar is a parable of things to come. The participatory consciousness is reaching ever-widening circles of interdependence. The rituals are becoming global. The leaders as well as the newscasting-priests will one day have to take on global responsibilities. Meanwhile, the exchanges of functions and services are being cast out like nets over the earth—medical, economic, agricultural, military, industrial. Participatory consciousness in domestic or global terms is a reflection of the participatory reality of this technological web.

We can understand the ambivalence of the participatory consciousness when we see it as a refraction of a material web of technology, because technology estranges even as it unites. Technological functions and services are objective and impersonal. We do not directly experience our dependence upon the rubber worker, the miner, the grapefruit picker, the air controller, the garbage man, except in crisis. After the crisis has passed, the sense of dependence quickly fades. There is no full human encounter to sustain it. Technology binds the world together in an invisible web of objective functions. In the human sense, this objectivity estranges even as it unites.

In addition to the estranging character of the technological web, our American social philosophy further conceals the dependence which the material web creates. The irony is that the nation which has done more than any other to create the technological order refuses to acknowledge the interdependence which it has fashioned. We live more out of our folklore of individualism than in the reality of our new world. We view economic organization as a private sphere, yet our industrial empires, closely intertwined with the political order, are more powerful than some nations. On economic and political matters, we make unilateral decisions which have ramifications throughout the world. We have created a society in which every citizen depends upon a web of services which he could never afford or provide, yet we speak and think as though each man or woman had to make it on his own. Many of our universities are huge financial enterprises, yet they think and act as though their decisions were private and no affair at all of the communities in which they are placed. Our educational institutions are interwoven with vocational opportunity and technical preparation, yet faculties and administrators talk as though the intellectual life were a thing apart from power and economic reality. Our university faculties carry on a multitude of private enterprises of consultation and publishing as "intellectuals," yet the challenge by students for a voice in these affairs is answered in terms of a folklore of academic independence and individual research. We conceal with our ideology and institutions the new social reality which we are creating.

The nation-state in an era of nuclear power is a parable

of the contradiction in our contemporary life. Once nuclear fission had occurred and this new power, like all technology, had become portable, our world was bound together in a survival pact. Each of the great nuclear powers could destroy the other but would probably destroy itself and the world in the process. The dreadful world of nuclear deterrents and the escalating costs of ever more complex nuclear weapons and missiles came into being. The power of nuclear destruction created a dependence of nations upon one another which the institution of nation-states could not sustain. Citizens contributed increasing amounts of their wealth to these nation-states for protection, only to find the very existence of their world in jeopardy. The material web of interdependence created by nuclear power had far outstripped the institution of nation-states, yet the folklore persisted that the nation is essential to man's freedom and well-being. The nation is about as relevant to our new social reality as individual enterprise is to the reality of industrial organization. Nevertheless, the folklore continues to cloud our understanding of the new social reality. The invisible web is concealed further by the refusal to recognize this new reality.

The Apollo moon-landing illustrated the archaic mind and institutions which we bring to these new technological achievements. The moon-landing was the cumulative result of work on rockets, propellants, electronics and astrophysics by scientists and technicians from many countries. The tracking of the operation was carried on from sites all over the globe. The science, technology and operation of the moon-landing were global through and through. Moreover, this landing was a harbinger of space activities which will knit terrestrial concerns even more closely in the future. Nevertheless, the United States treated the moon-landing within the traditional scheme of "who got there first with the most." The substance of the event is concealed by these shadows of an earlier epoch.

We encounter an alienated mind at the very center of the participatory consciousness. We sense epochal events of global unity coming to pass in the moon-landing, but we think of these events in the outmoded form of individualism, free enterprise and nationalism. The divided consciousness of the new world arises from a sense of belonging together and yet thinking of ourselves as isolated individuals called upon to make our way by private initiative. We shall see later that the younger generation is most deeply infected by the participatory consciousness and thus most intensely offended at the individualistic mind of their elders. However, the divided consciousness would not pose such a serious obstruction to the new social reality if it were not grounded in a fundamental alienation at the base of the society. Our institutions simply deny the actual interdependence which we have created with the new technology.

The divided consciousness is exploding in "urban riots," "rebellions" or whatever one wishes to call them. We gain some sense of the depth and power of the contradiction between participation and estrangement when we see its expression in this destructive form. Let us trace briefly the impact of the media on the ghetto resident from his sense of exclusion to acting out the society's own inner contradiction.

Ghetto dwellers participate in the rituals, dreams and promises of the high technology culture through the media. They too walk on the moon and celebrate the presidential homecoming. However, the nearness accentuates their distance from this glittering world. They know the hopelessness of job-hunting when education and technical competence are at a premium. They know the frustration of inadequate welfare checks. They live the vicious circle of poverty, bad health and crime. Alienation, exclusion and estrangement from the American world are intensified by the sense of other people's participation, belonging and membership. The appetite to participate is whetted, while the sense of alienation is exacerbated. Such mixed feelings come to expression in movements to enhance participation and movements to reject participation on behalf of separate development. When riots sweep the ghetto, men and women who never stole waken the next morning to find a new television set in the living room, as happened in Detroit. Many, if not most, returned these sets when the Detroit police recognized the irrational expression of feelings let loose in the rioting. That deep ambivalence of wanting to participate and knowing one's exclusion came into open conflict. The angry frustration at being excluded took the lead for a moment. The deep contradiction in American society came to expression in the collective reaction of rioting, looting and then returning the plundered goods. Participation was the key. Exclusion was the bitter reality. The rioting was America agonizing in its divided consciousness.

What is at stake here is a wholly new basis for membership in American society. Technology creates new terms of membership and participation, which we have failed to recognize and institutionalize.

What It Takes to Belong

In a high technology society, one either belongs at the outset or one is out for good. One starts inside or he never starts. Such are the terms of membership in the technically competent society. Without health, intellectual preparation, personal discipline and many other qualities, the opportunities of a high technology society are closed. The ceiling is zero. There are, of course, critical points of transition in which reeducation can occur. Experiments along these lines are being tried. But the prospects are limited and the resources are not likely to be allocated in this direction. The distance between the included and the excluded grows at an accelerating pace. This is true both within the high technology societies like our own and between technically competent societies and other parts of the world.

Utter dependence upon resources and services for membership in the new society contrasts sharply with our earlier experience. This dependence changes the condition of freedom. When we speak of freedom, we usually mean freedom to choose, to exercise initiative, to act in a self-determining capacity and to operate without undue external constraint. Being free, self-determining individuals and being Americans were once a single reality. We earned membership in the society by our initiatives. We found our way and reaped the rewards which were coming to us. We allowed for limited initiatives from government, but we did not trust them. What the individual did on his own was by definition good! What was done by collective power was a necessary evil!

Participation in the good life meant opportunity to work out one's future. The pursuit of happiness was an open road for individual development. One's worth as a person was recognized and supported by assurance of scope for individual initiative. Good space was open space! Anything that limited or restricted was bad! America was a land of opportunity—not as a place where things were handed out but as a place where individual initiative would win its reward.

Technological society changes the conditions for membership in a radical way. The pursuit of happiness now depends more upon external resources and services than upon inner drive. The game is changed. Personal, communal, cultural and social resources are now the prerequisites for happiness. It is no longer merely a question of removing the restraints which limited personal development, but of how to allocate resources in such a way that every person can participate fully in the society and be free for the pursuit of happiness. We now read "freedom for" rather than "freedom from." Without a broad floor of support *for* the pursuit of happiness, liberty is empty. This is the meaning of membership in a high technology culture. To be a member is to come within the care, nurture and resources of the technically competent society at the outset. It is to share the "interdependence."

The folklore of individualism, of course, misleads us about the American experience. Every person enters a culture through resources which he receives. None of us is independent in the sense that American folklore has suggested. On the other hand, certain cultures encourage individual initiative more than others. Certain periods in a given culture can be more open or closed to individual initiative than others. This is the way in which American individualism can be interpreted. Undeveloped land, emerging industrialism, a democratic experiment, furnished a relatively open situation for the individual pursuit of happiness. The folklore persists, although circumstances have been transformed by high technology.

Our increasing dependence upon educational facilities is an example of the changed conditions of a technological world. Education played an important part in American development—certainly from the mid-nineteenth century onward. Yet education was relatively rudimentary. Professional training was gained largely through apprenticeship. With the emergence of science, technology and complex organization, an increasing premium was placed on higher education. The lesson of this familiar story is often overlooked. Participation in society today requires training in linguistic, mathematical and cultural skills. School facilities, texts, laboratories, well-trained teachers and high-caliber administrative personnel are all ingredients of such training. When James Bryant Conant discovered the slum in the course of his investigation of secondary education, he realized that a large segment of the population was simply being written out of the society. He perceived that there would be no way back into the society for those slum children. Education today is too highly organized for latecomers. The pursuit of happiness depends upon belonging from the outset. Invitations to the pursuit of happiness conveyed in the media become frustrating and demoralizing when they are not accompanied by technical resources to give them substance. The ghetto alienates its people from the participatory society so long as ghetto residence means overcrowded schools, harassed teachers and "death at an early age."

We can now give a little more substance to the discussion of interdependence in a high technology society. We spoke of the material web of interdependence. Now we perceive the corollary in our dependence upon resources and services for membership in the society. We are not only bound to one another in a network of mutual services from day to day, but we are all dependent upon resources which only the society can furnish. Before we begin to participate as individuals we have to be included by the society. Some families are in a position to furnish resources for their children—witness the facilities available to suburban schools in contrast to ghetto institutions. Now, however, the denial of facilities to the ghetto means that one whole segment of the community is counted out. They are denied membership in the society. And this is over and above the tragic racial division which has plagued America from the start. The ghetto resident pursues a pariah existence on the margin of the culture. He never receives his birth-right for the pursuit of happiness. The media evoke the promise but the society refuses the fulfillment. The excluded thus become victims of America's divided consciousness.

To be free in a high technology society means first to share the resources and services requisite to membership. The pursuit of happiness presupposes certain conditions. Such resources do not guarantee a happy life, but one cannot pursue happiness in this kind of society without them. To be free is no longer a matter of removal of restraints on individual initiative. To be free now means being empowered by the society to participate. This is the significance of the new preoccupation with participation. The notion that one's family rather than the society is the source of this power is less and less tenable. The role of family nurture is another matter and very significant. Without a sustaining family group or its counterpart— say, a *kibbutz*—human personality is stunted and impoverished. But the family now depends more and more upon minimal income, work, health care and housing to exercise its nurturing functions. The individual and his family have to be included first if they are to be free later.

The case of medical practice illumines this transformation in dependence upon technical supports even more dramatically. Technological developments in medicine have come to public attention through organ transplants, yet technical development in this field has been extraordinary for many years. Along with the development has come an ever-increasing cost of medical care. The medical profession has become more and more dependent upon technical facilities. The research facilities upon which their practice rests have long since been beyond the financing of private resources. Year by year, medicine has become increasingly dependent upon public funds for training and practice. Medicine is now a major, collective enterprise! Meanwhile, medical practitioners have by and large maintained an individualistic rhetoric from an earlier day. They have lobbied repeatedly against governmental interventions to extend care to the old and impoverished. The irony is that doctors have lobbied for the sanctity of the doctor-patient relationship while depending upon public funds to furnish the hospital bed and laboratory.

The contradiction in technologized medicine dramatizes the divided consciousness which runs through the whole of American life. We live with rhetoric and institutions which exalt individual initiative. At the same time, we increase our dependence upon public resources for minimal participation in the society. We weave an ever-tighter web of dependence, yet deny it in our institutions. We leave the pursuit of medical health to individuals, while developing a collectively supported medical practice.

Here, then, is a profile of the participatory society. Men and women become members of this society only if they receive resources and services which the whole society creates. They cannot earn such membership. If it is not bestowed by the society, they will never enter. Membership in this new society requires a relatively stable home, a moderate level of education, proper medical care, access to major facilities and in general all the conditions of full participation in a technically competent world. Where these conditions are not present, one is caught in the vicious circle of poverty depicted by Michael Harrington. One is either included at the outset, or he is written out of the society. Our dignity as men and women now depends upon being included in the technically competent society.

This new meaning of human worth was voiced in an interesting way by Victor Nazario, formerly with the Center for Documentation in Cuernavaca, Mexico. He noted that while citizens of the United States have put considerable stress on the rights to life, liberty and the pursuit of happiness as these were stated in the Declaration of Independence and found expression in the Bill of Rights, they have given little attention to the starting point of the Preamble to the Constitution—"We the people of the United States." Msgr. Nazario was not, of course, arguing against human rights but in favor of the whole community, which engaged in the revolution and made these rights possible. When we recognize a participatory society, we are affirming that the web of interdependence is giving new significance to the corporate character of American life. "We the people . . . " is taking on a new, comprehensive meaning. The "we" is no longer an upper echelon of colonial America who had a voice in opposing the King. Our technological order is creating an interdependent life in which "We the people . . ." means the whole community. The rights which America has fought to preserve and extend will depend increasingly upon the corporate responsibility of the American community. "We the people . . . " can preserve and extend liberty only by undergirding the life of every citizen with adequate economic, medical, social and cultural support. We have to become more than ever before "A People."

Thus we begin to locate the divided consciousness of American culture. Our technological achievements create a participatory society. Membership in the society requires a share in collective resources. Freedom and dignity depend first of all upon an endowment of resources and services which establishes a new scope to the phrase "We the people . . . ." At the same time, we deny our new creation, mouthing an outmoded folklore of individualism, lobbying for institutions which exclude large sectors of the population from basic services. We end up impugning the dignity and worth of large masses of our citizenry. We deny our dependence upon them and our common dependence upon the resources of the society. We live with a divided consciousness.

This division of mind is acted out in the riots of the

ghettos and the protests of the new generation. Although the young protesters do not always identify the sources of their anger, they sense that participation is crucial. They know that participation is being denied, and with it the dignity of many members of the society.

A HUMAN HABITATION

WE ARE IN the paradoxical situation of enjoying a technological capacity to fashion a livable human habitat while engendering filth, violence, disorder and decay on every side. We shall search out the deeper principles of technological order which generate these paradoxes in the course of our reflections. However, on the first level of reflection we meet an initial contradiction which invites our thought. High technology cultures like the United States of America, Soviet Russia, Japan and some West European states have created rational organizations of productivity and exchange superior to anything man has achieved in the past. At the same time, these cultures are destroying their own habitat and endangering the life support systems of the entire globe. Each new step in productivity brings with it a deeper disorganization of common life and greater violence to the environment. In all of this, the United States is perhaps the worst offender, both in scale of growth and in unjust allocation of resources. We have traced some of these difficulties to the false consciousness of American culture, which develops a network of material interdependence but denies it through a folklore of individualism. But common to all of these high technology cultures is a refusal to acknowledge the dependence of all men on a system of exchanges with the life support systems. This refusal means that the mutuality in all exchange systems is violated, technology operates on a principle of unlimited growth, and the exchange system becomes a one-way process of exploitation which can only lead to death and destruction.

A dramatic example of such destruction was given in a report on the condition of Lake Michigan which indicates that it will take a century to restore it to a viable condition even with massive programs launched immediately The pollution of our water and atmosphere is so serious that the Secretary-General of the United Nations took occasion in 1969 to warn the nations about this major problem. To be sure, America is not the only contributor to the pollution of our environment, but American technology is a pacesetter.

The painful facts about pollution are familiar to every informed citizen. The stench is in the nose of every inhabitant. Our population is increasing at a dangerous rate. What is a threatening problem in America is approaching disaster proportions in many parts of the world. We are now over our moralistic hands-off policy of the Eisenhower years, but we are far from organized action on family planning. Our polluted air is destroying health. Our polluted water is destroying sea life and entering the food chain to destroy bird and animal life. Our exploitative metropolitan development is destroying green space and leaving less profitable urban areas to decay. Our urban centers are poisoned by automobile gases and made uninhabitable by the press of traffic. Our transportation systems are dominated by automobile travel which gluts each new throughway as soon as it is completed. Our visual environment is polluted by neon-lighted strips. Our senses are violated by offensive sounds, smells and sights. Pollution is no longer a problem, it is a way of life.

We usually think of pollution as an unpleasant sight,

sound or smell. But we know that these are superficial evidences of the environmental violence which is destroying the life support systems of our globe. The pollution of lakes and streams is killing off sources of energy and food, leaving only death and decay. The corruption of the food chain by poisons, if it continues at its present pace, threatens to destroy food sources for whole populations. The dumping of wastes which cannot be assimilated into the natural systems means that our overpopulated areas will soon choke on their own productivity.

Our violence to the environment seems out of hand. Each attack by a conservation group or legal curb by a government agency meets twenty additional invasions of the environment which cannot be countered. The unlimited expansion of our productive system is simply overburdening our life support structures. So long as those common means and resources in which we all participate and upon which all of us now depend operate independently of the common good and common will, we shall fall further and further into disorder and decay. The network of mutual services undergirds our participatory society, intensifying our dependence upon one another year by year. And at the base of that material network is an environmental exchange system upon which our whole culture depends. The organization of our common life depends upon our recognition of that life support structure and our readiness to make it our common political responsibility. The deeper paradox of our technological system is its refusal to submit its operations to this common good, generating ever-new modes of violence and disorder.

If one needed evidence of our disorganization, he would only have to compare the fantastic organization of automobile production or the moon-landing with our handling of air traffic. When the air controllers finally called a halt to the worst conditions in the overloading of the

airlines, alleviating some of the conditions most dangerous to travelers and controllers, it became apparent that
the disorganization of air travel was verging on disaster.
But the new society is an interdependent web of functions
and services. Air travel cannot be brought into scale
without dealing with automobile, bus and train transportation; further, each mode of transport sets up spatial
problems. Air travel cannot become safe without adequate
facilities which depend in turn upon urban and regional
planning, policy and government. The formation of an
investigating commission does not mean that the problem
will be solved all in good time. Citizens cannot be protected from the pollution of air and water unless collective needs and responsibility are recognized and institu-
tionalized. Who is to expect and demand that private
airline interests jeopardize profits and solvency for the
well-being of the commonwealth which they are serving?
The commonwealth has to answer for its own interests.
The human habitation is threatened unless the commonwealth begins to answer.

Perhaps the first step in organizing a human habitation
—a dwelling place for man in the fullest sense—is to
recognize the new social reality. We are now dependent
upon resources and services controlled by massive organizations which are indispensable to our freedom, our dignity and ultimately our survival. The control and allocation
of such resources can no longer be left to chance and the
exploitative advantage of private interests. In some cases
the sensible solution may be total governmental administration, as is the case with nuclear power. It may mean
the development on regional and national levels of authorities which can control transportation and environmental
change. It may involve some mixture of private development and public control—increasingly the pattern in activities which impinge directly upon the public good. But
the first step is to discern the corporate character of the

new social reality and our dependence upon participation in common resources and facilities for the simplest liberties—even the liberty to breathe air which invigorates instead of poisoning—the Right to Life!

We have glanced cursorily at the environmental dimension of our habitation. However, the human habitation has many dimensions. We noted some educational needs of a technically competent society, a matter deserving far more consideration than we can give it here. Education for the pursuit of happiness calls for enriching experience, as against segregated schools, whether in suburb or ghetto, which restrict experience. For limitation to one cultural area inhibits adequate education for global tasks. Young people need opportunities for education and work in at least one other culture area, preferably one of considerable difference from their own. Education for the new world is an encompassing project over the global community. It is a lifelong process. Creative years of educational growth may well come toward middle and later life, depending of course upon adequate grounding in formative years. Education is the process of a people comprehending itself in its heritage, environment and possibilities. This is the heart of democracy in a participatory society. Our interdependence extends our responsibility as a people. If we merely pursue private interests—not even comprehending our world—a managerial elite will have to step in and organize our habitation for us. This is the short step from divided consciousness to tyranny.

Participation in the new society depends undoubtedly upon purchasing power. Here our traditional institutions are paralyzing us. The meaning of human life is still conceived in terms of productivity. We trace our economic success to this motive and fear any restriction on the drive to get ahead. Welfare and old-age assistance handle some of the inequities generated by this system. The casualties of the system get first aid. But we resist the notion that every member of our productive society has a right to minimal economic security. We refuse to say "We the people . . . ." The striking fact is that the group who resist the idea of guaranteed income are the upper middle classes who furnish exactly such a guaranteed income to their children. There are, of course, many mechanisms by which a high technology society could enable members to share resources. Whether one thinks of the guaranteed individual or family income, negative tax or guaranteed employment, in each case the issue is whether we are ready to say that our new social reality calls for sharing resources so that each may be free. Do we assume that everyone makes it on his own in a society in which it is perfectly evident that one can make it only if he has broad support from the start? If we recognize this dependence upon the common life, are we ready to affirm the dignity of every member of the society by allocating to him the necessary conditions for participation?

Our system of welfare payments denigrates human dignity in a participatory society. In a society of individual enterprise, charity was a grace for the weak or incapacitated. In the corporate society of technical competence, charity is an offense against man's dignity and worth. This is the lesson which is so hard to learn when one refuses to think beyond the folklore of individualism.

We have evaluated our human habitation largely in national terms. However, the new social reality is global as well as national, and its possibilities are subverted by nationalism. Scientists and engineers have been able to work collaboratively on geophysical and astral projects, though nationalisms have restricted such opportunities. However, the problems of habitation are global in scale. It is difficult to imagine what a guarantee of economic security means in global terms or what controls on population such a guarantee would involve. Nevertheless, the expanding web of interdependence is drawing every part of the globe into a participatory world. Those who are excluded will become increasingly a locus of disorder as well as tragedy for this world. What we have thought of as foreign aid will have to be reconceived as conditions of membership. Needless to say, thinking through the new global reality transposes present rivalries among national and ideological interests to a different key.

Space exploration furnishes a lesson from which we can begin to think out our common life as a world community. One consequence of technical competence is the extension of human control over environment, organisms and possibly societies. There is no limit to the realms which technical competence may aspire to conquer; at least, we are in no position to place limits on these possibilities. Man may dominate every part of the globe and possibly the solar system. The web of interdependence will be projected into space with potential military threats and increasing need for mutual aid. Competing nationalisms on this scale sap the resources of particular nations and create points of disastrous conflict. Year by year a common share in space exploration becomes not only desirable but essential to world peace. As our technical powers increase, we generate technical resources which must be understood as our common heritage. Our high technology society presses us ever further into a worldwide web of interdependence. High technology nations not only threaten their own life support systems but endanger all of life on the globe.

We are now overreaching the possibilities which we can presently imagine, but it is essential to comprehend the trans-American scale of the new social reality. Technical competence knows neither geographical limits nor cultural boundaries. When the Western World and later every part of the globe embarked upon the technological adventure, they set in motion the participatory process as a first step toward an interdependent world. In limiting nuclear testing and pressing for control of nuclear weapons we acknowledge this global interdependence. However, American folklore and institutions obstruct our vision of the participatory society and limit our commitment to one world.

ALIENATION THROUGH TECHNOLOGY

WE CONSIDERED THE divided consciousness created by American rhetoric and institutions. This inner contradiction in American life, so we argued, creates a paradox of disorder—the tighter the web of interdependence, the greater the alienation and estrangement. Objectively, our individualistic institutions prevent us from organizing a human habitation. Subjectively, our mind is clouded and our problems seem insoluble.

We have created a participatory network through our technological triumph; we now need a new social morality and institutions to give communal expression to that participatory reality. The root of our problem would then appear to lie in our social morality. Can we match our technology with a new social ethic?

But is not a social morality a spontaneous thing which should issue naturally from our new social reality? Why do we tighten the web of interdependence yet fail to bring peoples and nations closer together? There is every evidence in our urban areas and certainly on a global scale that the cleavages between rich and poor, Black and White, developed and developing areas, are widening. Perhaps there is a quality in the material web of technologically ordered life which estranges and alienates. Are we moving, in brief, toward more and more terrible conflicts even as we increase our dependence upon one another and upon the common resources of our world?

Unhappily, it seems that a new social morality will not emerge spontaneously. Technology achieves power through domination and control, but even as technology makes life more interdependent, it estranges by objectifying and controlling the relationship of man to nature, to other men and to his world. Objective and impersonal, technology is the rational ordering of processes for deliberate aims, bringing each relevant relationship into its purposeful design, subjecting that relationship to pre-designed control. Every unit—whether man or thing—has to be reduced to a calculable quantity so that it can be brought within the logic of technology. The power of technology depends upon extending the horizon of calculability. The alienating character of technology is precisely this reduction of the world to the calculable. Yet men and cultures resist being reduced to calculable entities. Thus in creating interdependence, the techno-society also alienates and estranges.

Our reflections are shifting, then, to the negative side. While recognizing the possibilities of a human habitation and the worldwide scale of our new interdependence, we scanted our actual estrangements. We bracketed for a moment the agony of the techno-society in urban disorders and world conflicts. Now the brackets have to be removed. We have to penetrate more deeply into the contradictions within technology itself, where we encounter the destructive character of technological relationships which unite but separate, integrate yet alienate. Technological society creates a participatory web with one hand, while tearing the fabric of common humanity with the other. Thus the participatory world moves inexorably toward deepening estrangement.

Technology dominates its objects—whether things,

men, women, peoples, worlds—reducing the object to the predictable, powerless function in order to control it. The responses of the object—its movements or answers—become feedback within the system; then allowances can be made and control sustained. The object is reduced to its *meaning for* the system. The lake becomes outlet for waste. The lake as stillness, beauty in the evening, recreational spot, border for a path—these dimensions are suppressed or translated into feedback so adjustments can be made by the system. Technology reduces its objects to elements in its project, reduces men to functions for its operations, reduces the world to a field for its exploitative drive.

Our initial reflection on the participatory society stressed the integrative power of technology. Though we lamented the divided consciousness and the refusal to come to terms with our interdependence, we took a positive view of this participatory world. From the outset, however, we argued that the participatory society generates its own estrangements. Our first reflection located that estrangement in the divided consciousness. We have yet to give communal form to the web of interdependence which weaves our common destiny. We have yet to live in our new social reality. We have yet to acknowledge that being free is first of all being a participant in the new society. Being free is belonging!

Even if we could generate a new social morality appropriate to the material web, our technological order would generate greater and greater conflicts. We need an adequate ethic, but we need more. We are not arguing against the goods which come to man through his technology. We are opening our reflection to the alienative power intrinsic to the best of technology. Unless we can comprehend this negative power and deal with it, our urban disorders will drive us into a tyranny of techno-control. A false consciousness breeds disorder and oppression.

We turn, then, to the other side of the participatory

society—the divided, antagonistic world generated by the new technology. We turn to urban disorders which seem to grow with our technology. This negative side of the paradox of interdependence and estrangement is not introduced to cancel out all that has been said about a possible habitation for man. We can think through that habitation in a technological era only by being aware of our need to go beyond technology to solve its problems. Technology creates contradictions which may generate new thought and institutions. The objects of the technological system refuse after a time to remain mere objects. They assert their humanity. They refuse to be one more input in a system which dominates them. They begin to challenge the system itself. Thus the alienative element in the technological order sets the stage for a participatory order beyond technology. Let us reflect on this creative response within the urban disorders.

CHAPTER II

The Alienated Society

AMERICAN SOCIETY SEEMS more unified and integrated now than in earlier days. Many of the conflicts between regions, ethnic groups and religious denominations have been resolved. The United States is rapidly becoming an organizational society in which elites can circulate from business life to governmental and university careers. The industrial network is homogenizing styles of life and residential communities. An expanding federal bureaucracy is extending common standards to highly diverse areas. Even religious bodies are playing down confessional rivalries. All in all we encounter extensive integration of American life rather than division. Hence it seems utterly inappropriate to talk about "The Alienated Society."

Our preceding discussion of the participatory consciousness stressed the common mind which the media generate. We also examined the widening network of interdependence which technology creates. We found the participatory society divided in mind but hardly in material order. We even anticipated a new social morality which could bring America to terms with its material development. To speak of "The Alienated Society," then, seems to contradict the actual integration of the organizational society.

The integration of our new society is rather obvious. More and more activities are brought under national standards, whether they be standards to measure the effects of specific drugs on public health or standards of performance to determine qualification for admission to higher education. Transportation networks, military organization, educational activities and scores of other enterprises are integrated into what are now called "systems." This shorthand term "systems" refers to any process which can be treated as an interdependent whole of calculable parts. Economic policy is developed on a national scale by treating the economy as a system and seeking to establish proper balances in its functioning. Any other set of activities, from weapons development to welfare, so far as its elements can be made calculable, is drawn into systems analysis and programming.

Systems development is integral to what we mean by a techno-society. Technological society seeks to expand its rational control of the world by applying constant standards and making the future more predictable. Integration in a techno-society is accomplished by increasing control over discrete activities, making them calculable elements in a system.

Once a society begins to develop large-scale organizations which seek to extend rational control over its various activities, its scientists begin to think according to systems models. The process becomes cumulative. Industrial systems extend control over the productive system and in time over the system of distribution. Then the planners and consultants develop models of the system which rationalize standards even more and bring new spheres under control. The techno-society bears an inner imperative to extend its own control. Integration of parts by domination and control is the guiding principle of the system.

But man is more than a part of a system: this is an implicit premise of our analysis. This premise can be tested by observing the rebellion against control which is spreading through the techno-society. When man is alienated from power over his own destiny, even when he is alienated by the most beneficent system imaginable, he rebels and fights to have a voice in his affairs. Man is, among other things, an agent who seeks to shape his future and make decisions on matters affecting his life. The American experiment grew out of precisely this struggle: particular men, at a particular time, demanded a voice in their own affairs. The techno-system which now dominates more and more of our lives is a product of man's attempt to gain control of his destiny—but that very system is stripping its subjects of any significant voice.

There is a peculiar paradox of integration and alienation in the techno-society. This encompassing system has to extend its domination by more extensive planning at each new stage of development, because the marshaling and allocation of resources in the material network of interdependence require systematic determination. This may be done by market mechanisms according to some theories or by central planning according to others, but, as Chapter I attempted to indicate, there is an inner necessity for societal and global allocations in the participatory society. On the other hand, such central planning creates managerial elites who take over the decision-making process, creating a larger and larger proletariat or Underclass for whom others plan. Even as the techno-society is driven to extend its integration of various activities, it is generating alienation among its citizens by taking from them their rightful voice in their own affairs. Thus the integrated society generates the alienated society; the system generates it own disruptions.

Words like "integration" and "alienation" are quite abstract. Even notions such as "system" and "techno-society" are abstract, and, however useful they may be as shorthand to pull together many discrete experiences in our common life, they leave us with a sense of unreality. We are experiencing the effects of alienation in the drive to gain local control over schools and to decentralize decision-making in many of our collective enterprises and urban areas. Man is asserting his right to have a voice in his affairs, even if he has to assert this right by protesting a model cities plan which claims to be beneficial to his community. We are also experiencing the paradox of integration and alienation in the attempts of planners and policy-makers to gain more control over the allocation of resources.

In order to gain some insight into this struggle for a voice in the techno-society, we shall examine the situation of the Black community in our urban areas. The selection of this problem is deliberate: the Black man has from the first been forced into alienation by the American system. He was brought to this continent in violation of his own agency. His right to self-determination was denied in practice and in law, and when it was recognized in law it was again denied in practice. Thus the Black man is symbolic of the alienation which has gradually appeared as the negative principle of the American techno-society. He is not alone in his alienation; indeed, we shall argue that his alienation is a model of the reality which the techno-society creates wherever it gains sway in the world. But in the struggle of the Black community to gain control over its own destiny, to regain its God-given right to a voice in its own affairs, we can glimpse the way ahead for all oppressed peoples under the techno-society. The freedom of the Black man and the freedom of man are of a piece in the struggle for liberation, even as the bondage of the Black man is a model of the bondage which the techno-society creates.

URBANIZATION AS A
RACIAL PROBLEM

THE RACIAL QUESTION is so encompassing that one is quickly lost in its history and contemporary ramifications, and so we have chosen to limit our considerations to the urban struggle. The racial question is not equivalent to the urban problem, but urbanization in America cannot be understood apart from the struggle of Black people to have a voice in their own affairs. Moreover, America will only come to terms with its urban problems and ultimately the alienation inherent in its techno-system as it begins to respond creatively to the struggle for liberation in the Black community. In fact, the fusion of the urban problem and the racial question is the source of the intractable difficulties which we are now facing in urban areas.

The conjunction of racial struggle and urbanization is in many ways a peculiarly American phenomenon. The racial problem discloses the depth of the urban problem. Urban planning constantly confronts this depth as counterforce to its dream of the techno-city. By the same token, the diffuse racialism which corrupts American politics,

industrial organization and police-community relations—
penetrating and disordering every facet of American life
—crystallizes in urbanization. Here the racial confrontation within American life is taking shape. This depth of
the American problem becomes manifest in the urban
question.

The Rights Movement of 1954–66 paved the way for the
urban confrontation, but the situation today cannot be
grasped in terms of that struggle. The Rights Movement
broke the ice and let the subterranean forces surface. The
center of that Movement was the intention of opening
American society to Blacks on a basis equal to Whites in
voting, in access to facilities, in opportunities for work
and the right to serve in public office. Integration of
Black and White was the moral imperative. Admission of
Blacks to full, first-class citizenship was the goal. Some
think now that this step toward integration was premature
and collapsed because other steps had to precede it. Others question whether America can ever achieve integration of Black and White. In any case, the Movement
collapsed and Black Power emerged. Integration lost not
only its moral power but also its appeal to the Black
community. Looking back, one could say that America
was trying to buy off the Black community cheaply with
gestures toward integration and equal opportunity. Integration cloaked the profound reality of division and alienation at the center of American life. The seriousness of
America's racial struggle—centuries old now and far
older than the democracy itself—was being hidden by the
Movement and by the apparent support of White liberals.

America had reached a new stage in fashioning its
techno-society. Racial differences were losing their significance; indeed, segregated education was presenting the
military with uneducated Blacks who were simply unfit
for the new weaponry and organization. In the technological order there was neither Black nor White, only competent performance or incompetence. Color was becoming

more and more disruptive to the spreading network of interdependent functions. Government, industry, military and education were developing universal standards in which color differences were troublesome and in some cases obstructive. The Rights Movement rode the crest of this wave of spreading technology. The racial issue would soon be obliterated. Let bygones be bygones! Black and White together! We are all members of the producer-consumer world, thanks to the techno-society, so let's march into that promised land hand in hand.

The cry of Black Power on Meredith's March in Mississippi in the summer of 1966 sounded the death knell of the Rights Movement. White liberals had bought the universal promise of the techno-society. They really believed that color made no difference. They were convinced that the common cause with Blacks far outweighed the pain of past injustices and the anger which repeatedly surfaced during the struggle. Black Power crushed this White liberal dream. It thought the unthinkable—that color did make a difference. Black Power laid down one, non-negotiable condition for participation in the new society—Blacks would participate as Blacks!

Black Power is anathema in the techno-society. Not only did Black Power kill integration as a guiding moral norm, it also crushed the hopes of the urbanologists who dreamed of programming the masses into the brave new society. The very idea of urbanology as a logic of urban organization reveals the predisposition of elites to manipulate the masses toward the efficient new city. Integrative proposals for urbanization ran head-on into Blackness. And Blackness had allies in various ethnic communities who also resisted being programmed out of their communities into the new society. Black Power is not an isolated phenomenon obstructing the fulfillment of the techno-society. Black Power speaks to an alienative element at the heart of the new society. This is why the Black struggle can illumine the American situation. Black Power drew on centuries of suppression and alienation in bringing color and ethnic identity into contention with the techno-society. Where one ethnic community after another was being crushed by the urban juggernaut, Black Power raised up a community which refused to be programmed into extinction.

The urban question had actually been a racial problem ever since the urban migration of Blacks to the North in World War I. Black Power said nothing new in claiming that color made a difference. The new thing had been the attempt of White liberals and techno-scientific organizers to suppress the depth of the racial problem for the sake of organizing White America. For although alienation in the cities now has a peculiarly racial character which gives it explosive power, it is more than a racial problem. Our task, then, is to penetrate through the racial conflict to the trans-racial depths of urban alienation. If we can gain even a glimpse of these depths in the emerging society, we may begin to understand the alienation at the center of the participatory society. This alienation is not something special to Black people in America, but Black people have lived and felt it from the first as no other Americans except perhaps the Indian. Their story is then the depth of our story.

Two Urbanizations

AMERICAN CITIES HAVE always been divided. At least from the period of their significant development as urban centers, these cities were divided between the haves on the

outer circle and the have-nots in an inner core. This is
Richard Wade's thesis on our urban experience and he
argues it well. The suburban captivity of wealth and
power were writ small, then, in the early days of our
urbanization. This is no cause, of course, to assume that it
must always be so. Indeed, the alienation in our urbanization is now so disruptive that there is some question
whether urban life will be viable at all should it continue.
The new dimension in this division is the racial qualification of the urban struggle.

Divisions in American cities were for the most part
between newcomers and established groups. These divisions along social-class lines were qualified by ethnic
differences and cultural experience. From the time of the
large immigrations in the mid-nineteenth century onward,
group after group occupied the depressed core of the
urban areas and gradually moved outward and upward on
the backs of those who followed them. Some groups were
slower in moving, and some remained close to the center.
The overall trend was fairly uniform, however, and the
pains of poverty and endless work were somewhat as-
suaged by hope of deliverance.

America gradually developed an equalitarian ideology
which suppressed thought about social-class differences.
Social class was something associated with the Old
World. Whatever differences existed in the new land were
transitory and unimportant. Despite this ideology, however, our urban centers were laced with sharp social-class
differences and these divisions were usually qualified by
ethnicity. From time to time, especially in the course of
industrialization, social-class divisions erupted into open
conflicts. However, two factors mitigated the struggle between social classes: the opening of frontiers for emigra-
tion undoubtedly served as a safety valve; and cultural
barriers limited the organizational impact of ethnic
communities until they were already well on their
way to full participation. As Oscar Handlin has shown

in his many studies, we mistake our past if we overlook these deep conflicts between classes and groups in our history. On the other hand, we mistake our present crisis if we ignore its peculiar character, viewing it simply as a continuation of our urban past. A new, explosive factor has emerged in our divided cities, giving new and threatening shape to old divisions.

The two factors which ameliorated earlier conflicts no longer pertain. There are no open frontiers for Black people. In fact, there is no space even for a home and garden. Moreover, the linguistic and cultural barriers which blunted the impact of impoverished immigrants on urban areas—limiting their participation until they had developed certain skills by a second or third generation—do not really pertain with Blacks. To be sure, there are significant cultural differences and barriers issuing from centuries of segregated life in the rural South, but Blacks are American through and through; indeed, Blacks and Indians are perhaps the most American groups in culture and heritage. If Blacks are not participating fully in the new society, it is because something is wrong with that society. Of course, the urbanologists and White leaders make it their business to tell Blacks in every possible way that their difficulties on the urban scene are their own fault. They assure them that all will be well when they are educated or get adequate job training.

But these are only patent medicines of the techno-society. After job training there are no jobs. After schooling there is only the street corner. The ceiling is zero, so the mitigating factor of promised escape is missing. What had been an ethnically qualified struggle between social classes has become a radical conflict between a White Overclass and a permanent, Black Underclass. In the words used by Morton Grodzins in the 1950's when he saw this situation emerging, we face "the Metropolitan Area as a Racial Problem!"

We use the terms "Underclass" and "Overclass" in order to identify the *sui generis* character of our emerging urban problem. The polarized groups can be differentiated along traditional lines of economic life chances. The suburbanized, White ring is more established and affluent. The ghettoized Blacks are for the most part marginal in the economy. Lower-middle-class urban Whites furnish the upper classes with a bulwark against Blacks. The White ring is carefully insulated against contact with Blacks except when they venture into the urban centers to shop. Even then their principal contacts are with Blacks in menial capacities. The Blacks, in turn, are limited to a small area, and their contacts with the emerging techno-social organization are extremely limited. Most ghetto children, for example, have never seen a large office or any of a dozen settings in which the techno-society carries on its business. However, restrictions on life chances and social contacts have always characterized differences among social classes. The new element is the almost impermeable membrane between Underclass and Overclass constituted by the long history of racial estrangement. The alienation was not new. Black Power did not create it. Black Power only called attention to the social reality of profound alienation which the techno-society was suppressing. Black Power said there were two urbanizations and not one, so talk of "integration" was mystification. Let us heed this cry, then, and look more closely at these two urbanizations.

The problem was clearly stated by Alvin Pitcher in 1967 in his article "Two Cities—Two Churches," in which he anticipated the basic thesis of the Kerner Report. Mr. Pitcher stated the problem as follows: "There are two cities, two countries. There is a white city and there is a black city." He was particularly raising the question of how two churches—one black, one white—could heal a division in the cities, but his broader concern was to point up the radical division in our society. The Kerner Report later stated the same basic idea as follows: "There are two societies—separate and unequal." We do not mean at all to press fine distinctions in speaking of "two urbanizations," since both Mr. Pitcher and the authors of the Kerner Report were reaching for terms which would articulate the depth and seriousness of the division within the society. We use the term "urbanization" only to indicate that our whole society is going through a process— participating in an urban, techno-societal form—which makes the city an outmoded reality. However, we are also arguing that participation in this techno-society has been radically dichotomized from the start between Black and White. And, as the Kerner Report clearly discerned, the separation is worsening rather than improving.

"Urbanization" refers to spatial organization of the techno-society. It stresses the bounding of life space in areas of work, governance, communal intercourse, recreation and cultural opportunity. We have to recognize a shared urbanization through media and patterns of work. We already examined one aspect of this common world in the participatory consciousness. However, Black and White participate in this urbanization within distinct geographical areas. This is what we usually mean by ghettoization. The ghetto is at the least a defined, restricted physical space which limits egress and ingress. In addition, separate urbanization implies a distinct cultural and social experience. If urbanization describes our new social reality, then there is Black urbanization and White urbanization. There is a Black world and a White world. The Black Power Movement has rightly insisted on the recognition of this reality which integration concealed. Needless to say, some men and women of African ancestry participate fully in the White world, and, indeed, a few men and women of White or Caucasoid ancestry participate through marriage or personal affiliation in the Black world. Black and White are worlds and not colors. Birth is the usual but not the only means of entry into these worlds. They are distinct worlds—separate urbanizations —and communication between them is almost nil.

Black intellectuals and artists have portrayed some of the outlines of the Black urbanization. When Whites think that the splitting and rending of the society is not serious, they do well to read this literature. One thinks of the novels of Richard Wright, James Baldwin, Ralph Ellison, Claude Brown and many others who have come more recently upon the scene. One thinks also of the burst of insight from Black intellectuals in recent years as they have hammered out the profile of that other urbanization so alien to Whites. Reading this literature and attending to Black rhetoric, one begins to understand why Black students ask for Afro-American studies under Black control and why Black parents ask for control of their children's schooling. White urbanization promises only brainwashing for the Black consciousness, leaving completely untouched the problem of Black identity. White schooling reduces the Black consciousness to a social sickness, imposing Blackness as a stigma of permanent separation.

This is the serious meaning that can be given to terms such as "Underclass" and "Overclass." Would that these terms were not necessary in characterizing the two urbanizations! But we in White America are not dealing with a fluid class system or a changing composition of ethnic communities. The bourgeoisie-proletariat of European industrialization is an alien structure in our American experience; perhaps this is the reason Marxism has won so few recruits in the United States. We have two class systems—one White and one Black. These class systems are separated from one another in a hierarchy of domination and control. The White system is an Overclass controlling access to the techno-society. The Black system is an Underclass living on the edge of that White urbanization—participating marginally in its economic opportunities, spatially excluded from its day-to-day intercourse and culturally excluded from its hopes.

If Black urbanization is defined so negatively by exclusion from the Overclass and its White world, are we not wrong in thinking that the Black experience is a distinct urbanization? Are we not dealing here with a negation or privation? Perhaps this Black world is really a non-urbanization in a time of accelerating White development and urbanization—an arrested Black development, restricted from without through ghettoization and crippled from within through a stigma of Black inferiority.

These are the hard problems in urban policy and planning, hard problems for a Black urbanization. We are opting here for a positive Black urbanization, because we find in ghetto leadership, communal concerns of Black people, emerging community organizations, Black art, literature and thought and, above all, Black Power, every evidence of a distinct, promising Black urbanization. We also find that this projection of Black reality and possibilities expresses the basic needs and drives of all impoverished, excluded and subjugated peoples who exist under the hegemony of the White techno-scientific elites and managers. In brief, we are suggesting that Black urbanization speaks for the alienated subjects of the new techno-society both within America and throughout the world. This link of Black America to the Third World often seems a rhetorical device in Black protests, but our basic thesis is that Black America and only Blackness in America can articulate that subjugation and estrangement which techno-society is working on all mankind. The constructive lines of that Black urbanization have yet to be shaped in the Black consciousness, but there is more there than the White world can discern. Communication between the two worlds is broken. Until communication opens, the White Overclass is trapped in its own ignorance.

We need to give concrete form to our thoughts on this radical alienation in our society. The problem of broken communication may help us here, since we all experience this communications gap whether from the White or Black side. Merrill Jackson proposed a useful communications model for this Black and White separation at a symposium in 1967—a vertical diagram in which White is "Up" and Black is "Down." White is overvalued in the society. Black is undervalued. Here, as in our use of "Underclass" and "Overclass," we are referring, of course, not to authentic values but only to control of power and resources in the total society. Hence, in an egalitarian society, which is the America of folklore, Mr. Jackson pointed out, the relationship of Black and White would be on a horizontal line of equal exchange. Ups and Downs then contradict the basic ethos of egalitarianism.

Ups and Downs have a special meaning for communication. They represent a power model—a model of domination. This means that communication is screened through a narrow channel of stereotypes and informers on both sides. Whites receive messages from the Black world (the Downs) only in terms of their control mechanisms, stereotypical images and agents. Blacks receive messages from the White world (the Ups) only through the selected agents of that Up world. Since the discrepancy of power is considerable, the Downs seek to conceal many things from the Ups, and the Ups in turn refuse to hear or see many things which they should know about the Downs.

There is a significant difference in insight and understanding which comes from being on one or the other side of this unequal communications structure. Downs have an important economic and political interest in observing the Ups very carefully and reading possibilities for advantage or survival. Ups, on the other hand, tend to screen out unpleasant realities about the Downs—attitudes, gestures, etc., which might communicate dissatisfaction or hostility. Since the Ups have the power and the arrogance which accompanies such unqualified domination, they can afford to fantasy the contentment of the Downs. Many White southerners probably sincerely thought their "Nigras were happy," because they screened out perceptions of other realities. The Ups and Downs model, then, gives a radically asymmetrical flow of information and knowledge. Ups perceive and understand what they want to know to perpetuate their exploitation and what they need to know to justify undervaluing the Downs. The Downs perceive what they have to in order to survive "under the boot" and preserve their dignity by seeing through the hypocrisy of the Ups. Translating this model in terms of Blacks and Whites, one would say that Blacks could really tell the White world about itself from the perspective of the Downs and, conversely, that Whites will know and understand very little about Black urbanization except as it is expressed by Blacks in their literature and protests. Another implication of the model is that we need interpretation of this situation from both Black and White thinkers and movements. The asymmetrical structure of Ups and Downs implies that neither side can give a full picture of the situation.

The communications model of Overclass and Underclass or Ups and Downs implies that information passes upward from below through informants and is screened through stereotypes. The Overclass has the power to filter its information. That is what it means to be "up." The vertical power relationship, in other words, means that the Ups define the situation and the Downs are defined by it. So far as power, communication and access are concerned, this is the way information is controlled. Whites get information about Blacks through police, lawyers, judges, schoolteachers, social workers and some Black spokesmen who are *persona grata* in the White city. Whites are informed by their agents. However, even this information is screened by media through stereotypes which define the Black Underclass—lazy, violent, drug addicts, immoral and happy-go-lucky! On the other hand, Blacks receive messages from the White world through agents such as teachers, policemen and ward politicians. Here again stereotypes operate and are reinforced by the kinds of spokesmen who end up dealing with Blacks for the White Overclass. The Blacks experience exploitation and domination by an occupying force from the White world. Whites meet Blacks in menial roles. If Whites encounter Blacks in equal roles, they usually say, "Why, you'd never know he was Black!"

John Fry of the First Presbyterian Church in Chicago wrote a paper, "The Breakdown of Democracy in Woodlawn," in which he interpreted some of the images of the White world as they are transmitted in the ghetto. Like currency, symbols change meaning from one society to the other. Police who symbolize law and order in the White city communicate brutality and graft in the ghetto. The ballot box in which each person counts for one in the White city is experienced in the Black city as machine corruption where anyone's vote can be bought for a dollar. The school which symbolizes opportunity in the White city symbolizes defeat in the ghetto; the school is where you are told that you will not make it. And on and on—the symbols of democracy are transmuted to signs of corruption, violence and despair in the ghetto. Thus we grasp in dramatic form the meaning of two societies—separate and unequal. The symbols of freedom and hope in the Overclass world are transmuted to bondage and despair in the Underclass world. Thus we have two urbanizations—one of hope and one of despair.

Broken communication between the two cities means that legislation planned in the White world will be ineffective or destructive within the Black world. This is the insight of a former government specialist John Mac-Knight, who has worked on race relations. He pointed out that the power to legislate was held by the White community. This legislative process depends, of course, upon certain premises of what is the case and what norms will hold. The White power structure legislates from its own premises. It imposes its premises upon the ghetto in the form of programs. Consequently, the legislation misses the mark in the Black community. It may leave some benefits in the White community, as in upgrading White areas through Urban Renewal and dislocating Blacks, or may become destructive in the Black community, as in Aid for Dependent Children which undermined family life and Public Housing which created un-neighborhoods. This is an important insight, because it draws out the destructive power of the Overclass in the Black world. Even when legislation is presumably motivated by good intentions, the Ups cannot legislate for the Downs without destructive effects. Unless there are shared premises—a common city—the power of the Overclass undermines and destroys the well-being of the undercity. In a sense, every act and decision in the White city indirectly or directly damages the Black city. White urbanization thus comes about at the expense of Black urbanization, as we have seen in Urban Renewal, schooling and economic development.

"TELLING THE WHITE MAN ABOUT HIMSELF"

WE CAN INTERPRET the struggle between Blacks and Whites on the urban scene as a conflict between two societies, two cities, two worlds of radically unequal power. However, we shall continue to reflect on the com-

munications model which Merrill Jackson proposed, inter-
preting the disruptions in urban life as a struggle to
reopen communication. We are, of course, using communication in the comprehensive sense of encounter between
persons and groups in which identity, power and worlds
come into play. Communication in this sense is the total-
ity of man's interchange with his world and his fellows.

Charles Long of the Divinity School, University of Chicago, drew an important inference in conversation from
the riot in Detroit during the summer of 1967. He com-
mented on the distance between the White and Black
worlds, and then pointed out how thoroughly familiar
Black people were with the ways and identity of the
White. He referred to the early years of experience, particularly in the South, where Black children learned the
White man's ways for their own survival. Then he noted
the asymmetry in this situation, since the White is relatively unfamiliar with the Black and, in fact, rarely no-
tices or sees him. This insight is reminiscent of the title of
Ralph Ellison's fine book, *Invisible Man.* In this frame-
work, Mr. Long proposed that the riots, whatever else
they represented, were a way in which Blacks were ad-
dressing Whites. The disruption and disorder of our
urban situation, in one aspect at least, can be understood
as an attempt by the Black world to confront the White
world—to break through the barriers of agents and informers, stereotypes and managed news. Disruption is one
way to tear aside the Color Curtain which separates the
two urbanizations.

Without belaboring Charles Long's insight too much,
we have to acknowledge that the riots in Watts, Detroit,
Chicago's West Side, Washington, D.C., Philadelphia and
many other places were the only significant breaks in the
curtain which separates the two societies. Unfortunately,
Whites did not learn much about themselves in the process, but they gained some sense that things were not
right. They sensed that the situation was not viable, though

to this day the Commission's Report is gathering dust. To some extent the White man was hearing that all was not right with his city, and indeed with the future of American urbanization.

In breaking the communications barrier, the Black can be heard, seen and recognized. Telling the White man about the real situation has a reciprocal side—being seen and heard as the one who tells. Hence, telling "The Man" is also gaining visibility. In telling "The Man," Black was becoming visible.

We are not suggesting that riots, disorders, political struggles and social conflicts are in any simple sense rational or calculated strategies of communication. We are only drawing the inference that telling "the Man" is a communicative strategy of great significance in the confrontation between the two cities. Until "the Man" hears, the only possibility is two cities at war. Violence is the first step in communication between Overclass and Underclass, White World and Black World, City of Affluence and City of Poverty. We have no future as a participatory society except through confrontation and conflict, because we cannot participate in a divided society. "The Man" has to be told. "The Man" has to hear. Until that happens, he will continue to exploit, legislate, harass and suppress every agency or force which contradicts his stereotypes. (The implications for world policy and Latin America are all too obvious!)

It is striking that Malcolm X in his *Autobiography* formulates this task of telling "the Man" in clear and explicit terms. After he became a follower of Elijah Mohammed in prison and began to educate himself, he spoke of the consuming passion of his life: "It was right there in prison that I made up my mind to devote the rest of my life to telling the White man about himself—or die" (p. 185). This is to say that Malcolm X had begun to discover his own identity as a Black man, yet the process of bringing that identity to realization included bringing the White man to himself. There is a reciprocity in human relationships which means that my identity becomes clear and authentic only in the context of understanding and clarifying the true identity of others and particularly those others who are significant to me. In the divided world of Black and White, the distorted identity of Black Underclass cannot be overcome without dealing with the false, exploitative identity of White Overclass. This reciprocity of identities binds Black and White in a common history, so the fulfillment of White urbanization cannot come about without realization of authentic Black possibilities. Malcolm X's passion for truth about himself as Black and about the White man may not have included such long-term conceptions of human fulfillment, though toward his last days he seemed to be moving in this direction. However, Malcolm X grasped the ground of this conception in his insight that his own truth had to be stated in bringing the White man to truth. To open communication is to bring into the light—to make visible. It is "telling it like it is!" And this means telling "the Man"!

Rioting, looting, burning and sniping hardly seem suitable strategies for opening communication and bringing identities to light. However, these urban disorders, if the use of the term "disorder" is not too prejudicial to understanding the real nature of the events, occur as confrontations between two societies that are walled off from one another. The ghetto has witnessed year after year of complaint, demand, hopeless entreaty and broken promises. Disorder is bred by ghetto life. Police are not a source of order in the ghetto. They are a force which suppresses protest and imposes the exploitative order of the White world. Police enforce and perpetuate disorder in the ghetto, because disorder is essentially injustice.

Against such injustice, what strategy would the White

Overclass propose? A strategy of sitting down and reasoning together? That strategy merely perpetuates the White consensus, and even those who reason together end up as selected agents of the Overclass. Have we created two urbanizations which can only communicate through violence? Have we not created this violence from the start, from the day of slavery and through every step of subsequent discrimination and segregation? Can the false relationships of Overclass and Underclass, Ups and Downs, come to true equality unless Ups begin to discover their powerlessness to control the Downs? Can the Downs really find their true identity as people of worth and dignity without putting the Ups down? If one drops the Freudian concepts which sometimes give Frantz Fanon's thought an irrational cast, one can affirm his basic insight that the exploited cannot come to themselves without violent confrontation with the exploiters. Put another way, the Overclass has done violence day by day to the Underclass for three hundred years. The violence is not new, then, but is being communicated after all these years to the White consciousness. It is becoming visible.

BLACK POWER AND WHITE POWER

OPENING COMMUNICATION ALWAYS involves power. This is true between persons, groups or collectivities. To invoke another person's attention is to invade his power. Our attention is our power. It is our attending to the world which gives us a world. The world we have is the world we care about. The other person is only there for us in our listening. The importunity of speech lays a claim upon our care and attention. Our attention is our power of having a world. It is also our freedom to turn away from others. This freedom to attend or turn off is the infuriating otherness of children whom we think we can control or program. Children may retreat further and further into a private world of fantasy under excessive parental control, but they can and do exercise the power of attending or not, and this power is beyond our reach. To be a person, to be free, is to have the power of attending or turning off.

Thus, we would stress the significance of power in every communicative act, recognizing that our speaking invades another's space and forces him to make the decision to listen or turn us off. Even imposing the decision to attend or not becomes a mode of exercising power in the communicative act. And in this respect, presence is itself a communicative act. Our very presence places the other person in a position of ignoring or noticing us. Here our language is very illuminating. We speak of "noticing" someone, and in literature so much is made of "being noticed." The power of presence is its weight upon another's attention.

Black Power can be read as the emerging visibility of Black people on the American scene. That may seem an absurd way to describe Black Power when one reckons that the term was not mentioned until Black protests had shattered the equanimity of the White community. Certainly Black visibility had been emerging for some years. However, the term "Black Power" and the vagaries and insights which have flowed from it express the whole new situation between the two societies. The Black Underclass now define the situation for themselves, by force and violence if necessary, so that the confrontation between Black and White can be two-way. No more one-way communication!

We remarked earlier on the "invisibility" of Blacks to

the White Overclass. We also noted the power of the Overclass to define the situation in their terms. When Black Power emerged, the unilateral definition of the situation ended. Whites could no longer screen all information about the Black city through their selected agents, fitting the data to their stereotypes. Blacks were emerging in the Black world who would speak from within the Black community and "tell it like it is." The telling and the power are inseparable, for telling it like it is means that one has the power to define the situation and others have to contend with that new definition.

Remember the dismay and resentment with which the White Overclass reacted to the slogan Black Power! This reaction deserves more careful scrutiny than we can give it here. A whole history of White suppression came to light at the mention of Black Power. The ethos of White urbanization was finally challenged by an alien power. The Underclass had the gall to question White control.

White resentment and anger at Black Power stemmed partly from the false White consciousness. White folklore pictures American life as a free play of individual interests which are adjudicated according to rules of the game. Power is not recognized in this folklore. This false consciousness was manifested by administrators and faculties during student protests. Students sensed their powerlessness and tried to force the authorities to negotiate with them by occupying buildings and disrupting classes. The authorities argued that educational institutions were operated by rational discussion. Power, protest, violence, were simply inappropriate. Rational discussion and not power defined the terms of discussion in the university. Actually, administrators and faculty wield enormous power over students—determining curriculum, setting standards, controlling their fate and future possibilities, expelling them on terms defined by faculties and rewarding them according to standards imposed by faculties.

This overwhelming power of the authorities was suppressed in consciousness. It was simply denied. Rational discussion alone ruled in higher education.

This digression to a university setting sheds light on the White consciousness. Our society has generated more external power over nature and more internal organizing power over man than any people in history, yet we think and talk as though our dealings were purely voluntary and our ends purely moral. We have cherished control in every part of life. We have venerated power. Yet we picture ourselves as resorting to power only under pressure from enemies within or without. One only has to review the public rhetoric on our Vietnam war to realize how completely our exercise of power over the fate of Vietnam has been whitewashed. We used power in Southeast Asia only to protect a helpless country whose freedom was threatened by Communism.

Another aspect of White Power contributed to the revulsion at Black Power. White Power has employed violence at every point where America's will was opposed. White America has a history of violence as the Eisenhower Commission has shown. For the White Overclass, control of the situation really means violence. However much this reality is suppressed, it is latent in the American mind. The history of this violence reaches back to the earliest days of slavery. This White violence runs the whole gamut in American life from police brutality in our cities to our treatment of American Indians to our glorification of a frontier heritage of sudden death and our merciless destruction of opponents in global conflict. American opportunities to impose White violence and American resources to escalate that violence make a frightening picture. That picture becomes evil to the nth degree when it is suppressed and then clothed in moralistic language.

A tragic aspect of Black Power has been its entanglement in the web of White violence. Stokely Carmichael,

H. Rap Brown and many others, who have lived under the boot of White violence, are caught in this web. Black identity, then, seems challenged to match White violence. Perhaps this confrontation was inevitable. Human relationships are reciprocal. We become who we are through our relationships. Thus violence breeds violence. Breaking through violence to new possibilities is almost impossible with this history. The destructive imposition of power upon others evokes a struggle to survive by dominating in turn. In this sense, Black leaders with the exception of men like Martin Luther King, Jr. and James Lawson, have not yet defined the situation in Black terms. They have borrowed the destructive terms imposed upon them by the White Overclass. This is not the end of the story, of course, but it is an important aspect of Black Power. For the moment, Black Power is a reciprocal of White Power.

The transition from urban riots to organized Black Power may yet open communication between the White Overclass and the Black Underclass, but there is little indication thus far that this has occurred. The principal reason is that the White Overclass has a lifetime investment in exploitation of the Black people. The White man suppresses awareness of the power which he exercises. He glorifies his heritage of violence but thinks of himself as a peace-loving, rational being who is trying to be moral in an immoral world. He can sagely argue that those Vietnamese had to be napalmed in that village for the good of a free world; thus, he keeps his moralistic stance. This false consciousness is not divorced from his self-interest, however, since he draws money directly or indirectly from proceeds of slum property, prostitution, gambling and drugs in the ghettos. Certainly much of this economic advantage is concealed, but it is there. The wealth flows day by day into White coffers. But perhaps more important, he enjoys the social power which issues from looking down upon Blacks. The Jews filled this scapegoat role for the Germans. To some extent Jews also serve as a target for the disordered minds of White gentiles in America. But the Black man has carried the big load of America's moral and spiritual sickness. Black Power challenged this whole complex of moral, economic and social interests in the White society. Black Power is a challenge because it exposes White society for what it is. Black Power unveiled the sickness of the White man. So Whites resorted to their usual projection on the Blacks and spread panic about Black violence. (So the purge in 1969 of the Black Panthers!) What better way to conceal White violence in the city! What better way to screen out the reality of two societies which Black Power brought to light!

How then can we speak of the transition from Black revolt in riot and looting to Black Power as an opening of communication between two urbanizations? We can speak this way only in the sense that communication between the White Overclass and the Black Underclass depends upon Black Power matching White Power. Until the Black community can define terms for communication, there will be exploitation punctuated from time to time with ameliorative gestures. Mayor Daley of Chicago was not above throwing a bone to a Black constituency. He only drew the line at independent Black political power in the city. As he often put it, we do not talk about power here, we all work for the good of the city. He should have added, "the good of the White city!" There is no sign that Whites consider Blacks a threat to their control. When and how Whites will be able to come to terms with real Black Power remains to be seen. Until such common terms emerge, there can be no choice but violence and disruption. The divided society is drifting further and further toward violent confrontation. Up to this point Black violence has been turned against Blacks. We have yet to see a real confrontation. But if no one listens, that confrontation is bound to come.

THE RIGHT TO A VOICE

URBAN DECENTRALIZATION CAN be understood in this frame-work of two urbanizations. We suggested earlier that leg-islation is controlled by the White Overclass, so that programs either leave a few benefits for Whites and miss the Blacks or actually destroy life in the Black commun-ity. Decentralization of control over schools, housing allo-cation, welfare, medical care and other services is the only way that Black communities can defend themselves against White legislation. The federal government recog-nized the importance of local control in the Poverty Pro-gram when insisting upon "maximum feasible participa-tion." Model Cities followed a similar line. However, local participation threatens political machines and White power structures. Resistance to local control has thus developed in the White Overclass. However, resistance has also come from the socio-technical organizers of the urban area. Urbanologists who claim to know what is best for Blacks oppose local control. Thus, the White power struc-ture has enlisted those who employ integrative criteria of the technocratic society. Technocrats see local control as resistance to the rational city of the future. So the techno-crats play into the hands of the White Overclass.

The Black struggle for local control brings into the open the basic struggle of the emerging Underclass of the techno-society. Here Black Power becomes bearer of the destiny of the new Underclass in America and throughout the world. We have delineated the historical course which brought Black people to a separate urbanization. Now we need to understand that Blacks represent a distinct urbanization for the whole future of mankind in opposition to the subjection of man by the techno-society. Blackness has no exclusive claim on poverty or deprivation. Blackness is not distinctive of the new proletariat of powerless subjects of the technocrats. Technology alienates by dominating everything including man. It reduces everything to calculable quantities in its programs. The techno-society develops highly motivated engineers to program everyone's life, giving the elite prestige and power in return for selfless service. Thus technical and scientific elites collaborate with managers to form the new technocracy. On the other side of the technocracy is the passive role of the voiceless citizenry. This is the emerging Underclass. The Black man is in the vanguard of this new proletariat, because his history brought him on the American scene in subjugation to White Power. He is the spearhead of the struggle against domination by the techno-society, because he has been segregated into ghettos and forced into a separate urbanization. He is bearer of this destiny of the new proletariat and spokesman for the Third World.

Decentralization may well become the central issue in the two urbanizations. Suburban communities have enjoyed some small measure of local control, though not nearly so much as they imagine. The small towns throughout America live with a folklore of local autonomy, but they are actually objects of control by regional and national agencies. Local autonomy is a myth in American life today. Local community has no substantive power to determine policy and allocate resources. Theodore Lowi has seen this very clearly and described much of our decentralization as a fragmenting of governmental power into bureaucratic and irresponsible authorities. However, decentralization in a sound sense means that communities will gain decision-making power over matters appropriately coming into their competency and affecting their interests. That is a very different thing from fragmenting power. It recognizes that certain universal criteria of professional competence have to be protected for adequate schooling or health. It acknowledges the place of comprehensive authorities to deal with such regional and national interests as transportation and communications; indeed, decentralization would prevent fragmenting of authority in the many governmental structures which now plague our metropolitan development. Techno-society depersonalizes man and destroys human communities when it transfers all decision-making power to the managerial elites in their bureaucratic organization. Schooling, welfare, health services, housing plans, neighborhood development, distribution of access in neighborhoods and innumerable other vital concerns of the community demand far more local determination than our White urbanization now projects.

This brings us to an irony of the techno-society which is astonishing in the light of our democratic heritage. The new element in the techno-society is the crucial place of communication. The information explosion is an aspect of this phenomenon. Space explorations are dependent upon the new communications technology. Allocation and distribution of goods and services, as well as production, will increasingly be organized through new communications technologies. The implications of this development for work and everyday life are very far-reaching. However, this development in communications is being used to concentrate decision-making in the hands of smaller and smaller enclaves of specialists. Organization of activities is becoming more and more the private work of techno-specialists in consultation with planners. The very communications technology which could be democratizing society beyond anything which we have known becomes a means to concentrate decisions in a technocracy. The specialists and managers become the Mandarins or high priests of the new techno-society, reducing major segments of the citizenry to passive consent. The technocrats then begin to create leaders through a public image, and engineer support for their programs. Decentralization takes its stand in the democratic tradition which has always looked with a jaundiced eye on the concentration of power in a few hands, even when those holding the power repeatedly protest that they are holding it for the good of others. Technocrats are as easily corrrupted by power as any other group which has assumed a divine right to control man's destiny.

Black Power may well preserve American democracy as we enter the techno-society. Black Power projects an urbanization which may strengthen human community and local authority in the new society. Black urbanization can speak for impoverished urban Whites, stranded suburbanites who fled urbanization only to end in the powerlessness of suburban politics, the new generation of thoughtful students, alienated ethnic groups and disenfranchised rural workers, to mention only a few groups in America who belong to the new proletariat. The Black community has a special role, since they are the vanguard of the New Underclass which is already worldwide. We could call this the Third World, but the terminology is misleading since the New Underclass dwells most prominently in the New World.

Black urbanization can be carried through only if Blacks define the urbanizing process in Black terms. Let us be cautious here: we are not proposing that Blacks pull White chestnuts out of the fire. White urbanization is on the edge of catastrophe, and it would be nice to have someone save the day. But what Black people do in this matter depends upon their own needs and the direction they see for their own liberation. It looks as though Black liberation may set the stage for a humanized urbanization,

and they do have some allies in this struggle for liberation in the heart of the White Overclass. These allies are
the protesting members of the new generation who find
the techno-society oppressive and destructive of the personal values which they cherish.

Black Power intersects with the protest of the new
generation, because the young feel the full impact of
control by the techno-society. They know that this society
threatens their hopes for a democratic society. Youth are
a kind of bureaucratic proletariat in the new society.
Sensitive young people realize this, as we shall suggest in
the following chapter. This is the point at which Black
Power and the rebellion of the new generation come
together. Both of these movements may contribute to democratizing the techno-society, but neither movement has
much power.

There would be no way beyond "The Alienated Society" if we depended upon Black Power and the rebellion of the new generation. These are not powerful forces
against managers and specialists. After all, managers control the media and will resort to more and more propa-
ganda if their hegemony is challenged. Black urbanization
on its own will then be only a harbinger of a national and
worldwide Underclass soon to appear.

However, technology creates an antithesis within the
Overclass. The principle of rational control affects the
elites who exercise the control as well as the subjected
Underclass. This alienation is psychic in nature. It is not
as harsh as the alienation of impoverished groups and
exploited Black people; it is an alienation of spirit, located at the center of the techno-society, in the hearts and
minds of some of its most gifted children. The parents in
the White Overclass find it difficult to dismiss the protest
of the new generation, not only because its members are
in many cases their own children, but also because they
themselves share many of these feelings of psychic alien-

ation. They too hunger for liberation from the deadening routine of bureaucratic organization.

This psychic alienation is a dynamic force which may furnish some leverage for transformation of the techno-society. Those who feel the psychic alienation most profoundly sense their common bond with the Black community and all exploited peoples. This is the alienation of those whom we have called the bureaucratic proletariat, the New Underclass. It is creating a force for social change which may give new direction to the society.

As we explore this psychic crisis, we are shifting the level of our reflections on the struggle for freedom in our society. Our initial reflection turned upon the struggle for participation in a high technology society which counts its members in from the beginning or excludes them permanently. This led us to an understanding of freedom as belonging or participation. We viewed this as a precondition for any other freedom in the techno-society. Hence, the struggle for liberation has to take participation in the resources and capacities of high technology as a first stage in any consideration of being free. But participation is only a condition for freedom, as has now become quite evident in our reflections on the two urbanizations. Unless man has a voice in determining the affairs which affect his interests, those affairs will not be determined in his interest. This is clearly the lesson of three hundred years of exploitation of the Black community. Being free is having a voice and being heard: this will probably mean some kind of federalism in the development of an urban polity. Local control or decentralization is no panacea in a highly complex, interdependent society. Nevertheless, local control should be maximized on all issues within the competence of local determination. Furthermore, sophisticated technologies of communication can be used to increase local understanding of crucial issues and local contributions to policy-making. At present, however, the media are concentrated in the hands of the managers, so that even the most responsible new journalism ends up increasing the alienation of various publics. If being free means having a voice and being heard, this establishes a different set of criteria for distributing control of the media of communication.

Both participation and having a voice are organizational levels of freedom. No matter how indispensable these preconditions may be for a democratic society, they cannot come about without fundamental cultural changes in the meaning and possibilities of the techno-society. The dynamic for this transformation already exists in the psychic alienation of the Overclass. Attention to that crisis opens our reflections on the cultural problem of the techno-society. That same drive for personal wholeness is present in the Black community and may ultimately lead to a humanization of urban culture. But we can perceive this struggle even more dramatically in the protest of the new generation.

CHAPTER III

The Crisis of "Soul"

IN TAKING UP the crisis of "soul" we are shifting our attention from the organizational problems of the techno-society to its cultural meanings. Culture and organization are inseparable, of course, since the ordering of society gives expression to meanings and values. However, the proposals of urbanologists are for the most part tinkering with organization in order to adjust people and processes to technological control. The "Great Society" program under the Lyndon Johnson administration, for example, was a magnificent juggling of organizational gimmicks without any substantive consideration of the problems of a democratic society. In fact, it is characteristic of the techno-society that it refuses to reflect on its own nature and ultimate meaning. The control exercised by the techno-society depends upon unquestioning commitment to the goodness of increasing growth.

Reflections on the meaning of the techno-society for man would be an ivory-tower occupation unless there were some basis in the culture for posing such questions. We could think our thoughts, but our pondering would be totally unrelated to the active course of events. However, radical questioning of the techno-society is present throughout American culture and, indeed, is widespread through cultures of every continent. Even the most remote island peoples know that the techno-society is corrupting their mores and threatening their existence with nuclear holocaust. Even the affluent in America see a step-by-step escalation of frightful weapons and concomitant deterioration of environment along with each advancement in productivity. And on a personal level, a profound spiritual malaise runs through every level of the high technology cultures. The organizational contradictions strike resounding chords in the personal moods of the new society.

Defenders of the technological spirit comment from time to time on the spiritual sickness of the new society. They propose various stratagems to reduce these debilitating conditions which threaten to cut the nerve of the productive community. None of the proposals is very convincing, whether one considers more careful breeding of population, improved leisure activities, more effective drugs or more diversified occupational opportunities. The techno-planners themselves are infected with the malaise. The more organized we become, the emptier life becomes. The more we produce, the more comforts we install, the more pointless the enterprise appears. And this is not a mood voiced only by the affluent, though only leaders in the Underclass are in a position to realize what a false hope is being held out to their communities by the dream of a surfeit of consumer goods. The price of productivity is increasing control and domination of every facet of life, including the personalities of the practitioners of the new technology. The technology which promises freedom and deliverance binds its objects and its practitioners ever more tightly in systems of control. Technology objectifies man, nature, cultures, worlds, in order to organize and dominate. This is its genius. It is also its enslaving and debilitating character. This impoverishment is experienced through every level of the high technology societies. It is producing a crisis of "soul" in techno-man—a crisis which infects not only those who are dominated by technology but also the dominators; and by "soul" we mean here the whole inner life of sensibility and spirit.

No contemporary writer has captured this sickness of soul in the technologized world more completely than Aleksandr Solzhenitsyn. His major works—*One Day in the Life of Ivan Denisovich, The First Circle* and *Cancer Ward*—depict the dehumanization of man in the technological society. His works have circulated in America somewhat as anti-Communist literature. However, he is as much a critic of American technological organization, at least in challenging dehumanization in the techno-society, as he is of the particular form this has taken in the Soviet Union. He is pleading for personal freedom in a world which violates freedom through domination from without and through terror from within. Solzhenitsyn, like many writers in his tradition, is pleading for the Russian soul.

Professor Hromadka of Czechoslovakia had a similar message for Americans in December, 1966, on a tour of the United States. In speaking of the dialogue between Christians and Communists which had slowly begun in his homeland, he told of the economic and material advancements of the society and referred to this development as a "House" which had been built in the post-war years. He

observed that Communists and Christians alike were ask-
ing about the kind of man who would inhabit this
"House"; at the very moment of realizing some of the
conditions for the Marxist society, even more fundamental
questions were being posed about the New Man in this
society. Here, of course, was common ground for dialogue
between Christians and Communists. Christians had failed
in the past to take social conditions fully into account,
but never tired of raising the question of man. One of the
tragedies of the Soviet invasion of Czechoslovakia in the
summer of 1968 was the suppression of these fundamental
questions. The question of man, the problem of authentic
human existence, has the most radical implications for
every society but poses a critical issue for the controlling
agencies of the techno-society. This is the question raised
again and again by poets in the Soviet Union. Liberaliza-
tion in Czechoslovakia had opened the door to these questions. Soviet fears slammed the door. And to be sure, the
question of man is troubling to any techno-society, because it is not simply a matter of building a "House" and
then discovering man. The man is formed in the building
of the "House." This is the deeper question troubling the
sleep of the technocrats as well as the soul of the
people.

The crisis of "soul" accounts for the strange paradox of America's growing affluence and rising rebellion of youth. In some ways post-World War II affluence
in America is the fulfillment of the American dream. That
dream included more than material comfort, but in a
special way America attracted men and women from the
Old World because it promised relief from the grinding
poverty of the new industrial age. The New World glit-
tered with promise of rewards. And America rewarded the
labors of many who sought this opportunity. Even taking
account of the deficiencies in this prosperity, and they are
extremely serious, the dream of prosperity is closer to

fulfillment in this land than anywhere in man's experience. Yet in this moment of realization, America is experiencing a radical disenchantment. The new generation especially displays a deep disaffection. The Black community evinces this mood in separatist movements. The most successful barely conceal their malaise. These are the outward signs of the crisis of "soul" which can guide us to a deeper understanding of the problems and possibilities of the new society. Were it not for this deep restlessness in the American soul, we would be well on our way to the controlled, bureaucratic order which Solzhenitsyn portrays so graphically in *The First Circle*. Like the dwellers in the first circle of Dante's *Inferno*, these citizens are neither good nor bad but simply go through the motions. Their life is empty. They do as they are told and utilize their capacities for the system. Unless the spirit of man rebels, and Solzhenitsyn records such heroic rebellions, this is the destiny that awaits high technology societies. But that rebellion is occurring on all sides along with the extension of technological power.

The crisis of "soul" is unevenly distributed in the society, evoking a more vital response in some sectors than in others. The careerists of the new society, for example, suppress their anxiety in many ways. They stifle restlessness by endless work, by expeditious use of sleeping pills and alcohol, and above all by continuous acquisition of material wealth and comforts. These careerists are to be found in industry, government, military, medicine, higher education and many other walks of life. The new technology feeds their particular sickness so they adjust rather well. Thus the Overclass narcotizes its malaise with activity. However, their children are in revolt, so they feel poignantly the disenchantment which they have kept at arm's length. After a lifetime of work, the Overclass sees its progeny in rebellion against all the values for which they labored. The new generation feels the crisis of "soul" more deeply than the parents, because they have not yet buried consciousness in careerism. They have seen the emptiness of their parents' lives, yet this disenchanted youth also expresses the spiritual uneasiness of their parents. However much the parents repudiate the rebellion, they recognize themselves within the disenchantment of their children. The new generation acts out the rebellion which has been suppressed within the Overclass.

When we take up the crisis of "soul," then, we are not examining an isolated phenomenon which is external to the inner genius and development of the techno-culture. The revolt is at the heart of the new society. It gives form to the malaise which plagues the technocracy. It gives voice to the groaning of the multitude who are being programmed for contentment. It even expresses the anxieties of the reactionaries who grieve over the passing of individual initiative and local control. But as always it is a creative, and sometimes possessed, minority who act out this protest. This appears to be the lot which has fallen to the rebels in the new generation.

THE REVOLT OF YOUTH

THE CRISIS OF "soul" is internal to the new society. It is borne by the children of the middle and upper middle classes. These are the successful in-group of the new society. Other groups share the revolt, as we shall have occasion to observe, but the talented children of the Overclass are leading the revolt against the values and organization which their parents uphold. The parents are not repudiating these young people unequivocally. In some cases parents have been very sympathetic to the protest. Certainly many young people are going along with the establishment, making their peace in such ways as they can. And in many cases parents utterly reject the new generation, although even these parents try to maintain communication with their children.

In general, the rebellion is not among out-groups who resent the affluent society. The disenchantment is among the children of affluence. This is the common element in the revolt. In other respects, the revolt is complex and variegated. It is anything but a unified movement. It is certainly not organized. Hence we collect under the term "revolt" such diverse phenomena as the new radicalism, the drop-out culture, the drug culture, the revolution in sexual mores and the new esthetic. This is a mixed bag. It hardly forms a revolt. American youth seem to have splintered into a thousand fragments. At the peak of its world power, America seems to be coming apart at the seams, losing control of its youth and dissolving into warring factionalism.

We shall treat these diverse forms of youthful revolt as a single movement, claiming that these are different styles of negating the techno-society. The rebels talk about "the establishment" or "bourgeois values." They see the techno-society from the point of view of the Underclass, so that "establishment" means those who program others. Young people are objects of the techno-society. Their abilities and skills are needed to man that society. They are being programmed from nursery school onward to take up their positions in the technological organization. They are trained in verbal, interpersonal and quantitative skills so that they can perform almost as well as computers in the new society. Consequently, the new generation sees the techno-society as a "power" shaping its future. Even though these young people may "make it" into the

Overclass, their existence as persons is impoverished by this programming.

The diverse styles of revolt can help us understand the crisis of "soul" in America, for the different styles bring particular aspects of the new society into question. The new radicalism, for example, is only one and probably not the most important challenge which the new generation is raising against the establishment. The same holds for the drug culture which frightens the older generation. We do well, then, to reflect rather concretely on these forms of protest. We should consider why these rather than other forms are appearing at this juncture of American history. Young people continually point out that their parents are not listening. Our first objective, then, will be to listen to this protest in its diversity.

One can listen too uncritically to protests. Protest is usually ambiguous. Protest arises against a particular reality and participates in the distortions of that reality. The struggles of the poor are burdened with the materialism of their exploiters. The Black struggle is corrupted by the exploitation and violence of its oppressors. Youthful protests are dependent upon the same drive for control which makes the establishment so oppressive. When we recognize the limitations of every protest, we are saying that the most complete negation participates in that which it negates. Anti-Communists oppose totalitarianism in a totalitarian way. Anti-capitalists deride the greed of entrepreneurs for the sake of material values which they cherish. And so the youthful revolt is itself infected with the struggle for control against which it rebels. These limitations in any protest do not invalidate the claims of the protesters, but they make us discriminating in our interpretation of the realities to which they are drawing attention.

The connection between the youthful revolt and the cultural crisis intrinsic to high technology will have to be demonstrated in our interpretation of that revolt. The connection is not self-evident. We propose it here as a guiding hypothesis. Even at the outset, however, the negation of technology furnishes a clue to the worldwide character of the youthful revolt. Many reasons, of course, have been adduced for this worldwide phenomenon. The growing numbers of young people are a favorite reason proposed by demographers. The availability of media is another reason congenial to the McLuhanesque approach. And undoubtedly technology does contribute the conditions for its own undoing, making possible the dangerous explosion of population and creating means to a common consciousness. However, material conditions may be necessary but are seldom sufficient to account for historical reality. This is particularly true of the worldwide character of the youthful revolt, whose only common element is the presence of high technology. Some observers, for example, attribute the youthful rebellion in America to child-rearing practices, yet we encounter such rebellions in Europe and Japan where very different practices prevail. Other observers try to see the youthful protest as an American phenomenon, but one encounters it in Italy, Soviet Russia, Czechoslovakia, Red China and parts of Africa. We do not intend for a moment to reduce these multifarious protests to a single theme. However, we do recognize a struggle for authentic human existence running through the whole gamut of them throughout the world; moreover, the protests grow in intensity, number and power according to the stage of technological development of the culture. The only exception to this is Soviet Russia, and there is evidence that terror drives all protest deeper and deeper into the crevices and hidden places of Soviet society.

We are proposing, then, that the youthful rebellion brings to light the crisis of "soul" which techno-society generates. We assume that this crisis is emerging as negation wherever high technology is gaining dominance. We claim, though we could not demonstrate it and will not try, that this youthful protest in the name of "soul" has its counterpart throughout the world in similar movements of youth and raises the basic question of human existence in a techno-culture. But above all we are arguing that understanding the rebellion of youth brings us one step closer to grasping the inner contradictions of the techno-culture.

The term "soul" has many meanings and little meaning for many people. We are not thinking of an eternal substance which distinguishes man as a creature of God. The idea of substance and the corresponding notion of soul are practically unintelligible to modern thought. We think now in terms of dynamics and process. Hence, we take "soul" in a more existential sense—the way in which man is related to his world. "Soul" refers, then, to the wholeness or integrity of man, his embodied feelings and sensibility, his struggle for an authentic existence and in general to the quality of his subjectivity. When we speak of a "struggle for soul" or a "crisis of soul," we are speaking of man's struggle for a style of life appropriate to him as man.

We interpret the rebellion of youth as essentially a struggle for soul. Two poles are discernible in the rebellion: a negative pole which expresses what Herbert Marcuse would call refusal to play the game, and a positive pole in which a new style of humanness is projected. The refusal is, of course, easier to comprehend, because it negates so much with which we are familiar in our techno-culture. Furthermore, the refusal has high visibility. It provokes deep anxieties in the older generation and in certain instances leads to violent opposition from the establishment.

Members of the new generation are constantly criticized for an almost nihilistic attitude toward contemporary so-

ciety. They are challenged to furnish some alternative to
the things which they negate. This is not a legitimate
criticism of the rebellion, because much more is postu-
lated in the new style than the establishment can see or
understand. We shall gain some sense of this new style
even in the negation of the technological ethos.

CHALLENGE OF THE NEW LEFT

THE NEW LEFT and especially such groups as Students
for a Democratic Society are modest in the scope of their
rebellion. Of course, the New Left think of themselves as
extremely radical. They are challenging the military-in-
dustrial-government power structure. They have at-
tacked major institutions of higher learning. They are
trying to strike up a coalition with labor. They are developing programs to organize the impoverished sectors of
the society. They have demanded that educational institutions take responsibility for the communities in which
they are situated, thus advocating a new localism amidst
growing corporatism. In what sense, then, could one possibly view the New Left as relatively modest in their
challenge? What about the new heroes like Mao and Che
Guevara!

Of course, there is enormous variety in the New Left.
They are at war within themselves. But the New Left
limit their negation to the anti-democracy of the American techno-society. As Richard Flacks has noted in his
researches, the New Left are drawn largely from demo-

cratic homes of the middle class. They are repelled by the coalitions of power which dominate the new society. They dream and work for a participatory democracy which can realize the promise of technology without sinking into the abyss of a managed society. They are disgusted with the corruption of the managerial class—material values, dependence on sedatives, bourgeois style and preoccupation with control. They do not want a New Man or even a New Society. They want to democratize the techno-society by giving everyone a voice and equalizing access to the material goods of the new productivity. (Here we pass over but do not forget a nihilistic element who are to be found in the New Left—viz. the Weatherman faction.)

Earlier spokesmen for the New Left like Carl Oglesby would of course argue that their protest is the true radicalism. Certainly the Progressive Labor Party split with the main body of SDS because it wished to pursue a more orthodox Marxism in contrast to SDS, which is developing a diffuse protest against all forms of anti-democracy in the techno-society. But the New Left have no more use for Marxist organization in the communist societies than they have for the American establishment. And the feeling is mutual, because Marxism has moved rapidly toward a bureaucratic organization of technology which has little room for radicalism. Participatory democracy is as abhorrent to Marxist societies as the individualistic democracy of the bourgeois West. SDS has ended up saying, "A plague on both your houses!"

If the New Left are discontent with America's techno-society and alienated from organized Marxism, perhaps they are more radical than they appear. How is it that we view them as a relatively modest protest among the new generation? The New Left are essentially moralists. The New Left took America's democratic values to heart, as Kenneth Keniston has noted. They absorbed the principled concerns of their families. They are thoroughgoing moralists. They want America to be consistent—to realize the promise of a democratic society. Consistency is the heart of moralism. It pushes universal applications. And this moralism knows no bounds! SDS condemns administrators, faculty, fellow students and competing movements which disagree either on objectives or methods. Right and wrong are sharply distinguished. Any ambiguity in judgments or situation is dismissed. The god of the New Left is consistency in a very inconsistent world. In this sense, the New Left carry the American ethos of achievement and the technological will to the nth degree. When the establishment looks at this New Left with horror, it is repelled because it is looking at itself in caricature. This is the moralization of the techno-society. It would redistribute power and goods without challenging the society itself. It leaves techno-man deeper than ever in his spiritual malaise.

The anti-democracy of the techno-society is challenged by the New Left. Yet movements like SDS sense that a redistribution of power, however just according to the principle of participation, leaves the society unchanged. They do not wish to hold the power, because they realize that this will compromise their purity and require all kinds of adjustments to the realities of institutional life. This deep ambivalence in the New Left stems from the fact that they are protesting against the society in the name of the very values and style of life which created the techno-society. In this sense, the New Left are a part of the technological order. They do not really challenge the notion of man as exploiter. Segments of the New Left who sense this basic contradiction in the movement take a nihilistic stance and propose the destruction of all institutions. This, however, is an abortive reaction and has little support.

The New Left accept the techno-society and the men who rule it, merely challenging that society to realize its full possibilities for the good of all men and to share with all men the decisions which affect their interests. Nothing could be more American than these hopes. They are the dreams of American democracy—the productive society become a participatory society.

In viewing the New Left as modest in challenge, we are not rejecting their criticisms and concerns. Our discussion of the participatory society explicated the ground for the democratic values which the New Left are proposing. However, the politicizing of a participatory society in mass movements, even movements of enlightened people, is a romantic notion which should fill any reasonable person with dismay. We have seen a catastrophic demonstration of such democracy in the work of the Red Guard throughout China. And this is the other side of the ambivalent challenge of the New Left. They are romantic in trusting their own motives. In contrast to the pluralism of styles and cultures toward which our participatory world could move, the New Left encourage mass culture under something analogous to the puritanism of the Red Guard. When we say the New Left take democratic values to heart, we mean precisely that. They are impatient with human evil and pride. They project this evil upon an older generation and its institutions, suppressing the reality that many of their leadership are already in transition into that older generation. And they obscure the limitations in their own vision, thus falling afoul of one another in factional claims to absolute truth. The absolutizing of democratic values in a single group thus becomes the subversion of democracy. The only voice to be heard is the true voice; that is, the voice of the New Left. And thus they end up in the camp of the techno-specialists who have the truth and are quite ready to sacrifice themselves in programming others into this truth.

If we reject the moralism and romanticism of the New Left, what is left in this protest to enlighten us? Here we have to draw attention to an earlier disclaimer! The fact that a negation participates in the reality which it negates does not invalidate its challenge. The New Left are part and parcel of the moralism that has always characterized America, giving a demonic quality to movements like Abolitionism and Prohibitionism and pushing America's military strategies beyond rational limits in "defense of democracy." Yet the peculiar task of this New Left has been to identify the anti-democracy of the techno-society, and their insights are extremely important.

The New Left have drawn attention to the one-way communication that develops in a techno-culture—which transmits messages down to the programmed and receives only such feedback as is appropriate to maintain control. They have detected the same process in higher education, where careerist faculty and administrators hide their intellectual entrepreneurship behind the façade of rational discussion and intellectual endeavor, exploiting their students and attending to their book sales and research grants. They have focused attention on the military-industrial-governmental-educational establishment so that even managers in defense-related industries are ready to discuss the problem. They have kept public attention alive to the growing segregation and impoverishment of selected sectors of the society. They have been and continue to be a living conscience to America. Sadly enough, they are the only consistently prophetic voice on the American scene. Religious leaders, Black leaders, intellectuals, the labor movement and political leaders from time to time raise issues in a prophetic way, but these groups are deepy entangled in their own vested interests and seldom bear a consistent witness against the anti-democracy of the techno-culture.

Hence, our reservations about the moralism of the New Left are proposed out of concern for the movement rather than rejection of it. Their prophetic witness is too important to America to be subverted by the same drive for domination which makes a techno-culture anti-democratic and inhuman. If one has to choose between a politburo, a military-industrial complex or a Red Guard, there is little choice. We need the challenge of the New Left, but the crucial problem in challenging the techno-system is to find means which bring the will-to-control into question without simply aping its violence and domination. The problem is to challenge the techno-will through means which bring a new man into being. In a cultural revolution, being heard is a beginning, but one must be heard in a style that anticipates the liberation which one brings.

THE "TURNED-OFF" GENERATION

IN DRAWING ATTENTION to the entanglement of the New Left in the drive for domination of a techno-culture, we have already raised the question of man in the new society. The nature of man and the fate of man in a techno-culture are the heart of the matter. We must come to terms with the understanding of man in the techno-culture, which is the target of the "turned-off" generation in its revolt against the new society. It is less concerned with particular organizational defects of the techno-society than it is with the fate of man in the best techno-culture. It is challenging techno-man and his whole enterprise.

Hippie movements, drop-outs, mass movements of youth and various esthetic movements are bearing this radical witness. We bring them together under the term "turned-off" generation, though they represent distinct negations and proposals for a new world. They have "turned off" the techno-culture. They negate technical competence as a way of life and mode of human fulfillment. They reject to different degrees the material comforts of the new society, because they recognize the enslavement that attends the consumer way of life. They reject man as producer. They surrender any claims to power in the techno-society, knowing that power is the other fellow's game. They reject the achievement culture and its activism. They seek a new man who enjoys his world and hears his neighbor. They seek spontaneity in contrast to the calculations of techno-man. They seek community in place of the bureaucratized order that envelops them. They are "turned off."

There is as much ambiguity in the revolt of the "turned-off" generation as there is in the New Left, though it is not nearly so entangled in the ethos of the techno-culture. In contrast to the relatively conservative drive of the New Left toward a participatory society, the "turned-off" generation is saying a radical No! to the techno-culture. It discards the neat clothing of the standardized techno-world. It neglects the hygiene which is so useful to an urbanized culture and such a fetish in its middle-class families. It rejects the "schooling" which programs the children of the techno-world. It refuses regular employment as a path to a career. It despises the trimmed hair of the office culture. It surrenders control over its life conditions and prospects. It becomes "down and out" instead of "up and coming." In every possible way, it embodies the antithesis of techno-man and his controlled world. This is an out-and-out repudiation of the Protestant ethic of a disciplined, obedient will which suppresses all feelings and desires for the sake of accomplishment in this world. It has cut the nerve of that ethic which inspired and drove Western techno-man to the domination of his environment, the natural order, the non-industrialized cultures and finally his own people.

The "turned-off" generation is as caught in romanticism

as the New Left. This faith in the primitive will endangers the young by making them victims of predatory elements in the society. This dream of the "golden age" of the uncivilized blots out the consciousness of evil. As Nicholas von Hoffman observed, the consequences in areas like Haight-Ashbury have been pathetic and cruel. The true archaic community is sustained by an intricate web of obligations and sanctions. Casting away the surface manifestations of the techno-culture in no way institutes that kind of archaic community. However, the attempt to rid oneself of the trappings of technical civilization discloses the deeper search for authentic existence in this new generation. This is the significant thrust of the protest, however limited it may become.

Preoccupation with subjectivity is the heart of the protest in the "turned-off" culture. It is searching for feeling and sensibility. It is breaking through the controls and inhibitions which dominate techno-man and make him such an effective manipulator of others. Its impatience with "schooling" also stems from this repudiation of rational control. We like to think of "schooling" in America as intellectual preparation, but much of it is programming for middle-class disciplines. Schools reward good performance, teach manipulative skills, develop capacities to handle words and quantities; then, they test the students on these skills and advance only those who are well programmed. The "turned-off" generation rejects "schooling" because it repudiates the competent man of the techno-culture.

The "turned-off" culture (subculture would be more accurate, since it is part of a larger youth rebellion) is a new mendicancy. It is the "religious" of the new generation. It may well be one of the few authentically "religious" movements in contemporary culture. Much like the lay mendicant movements which swept Europe from the thirteenth through the fifteenth centuries, laying the foundations for the Reformation, this "turned-off" generation is wandering over the world, exploring new styles of life and developing communities of various types. The Beguines, Beghards and Cathari were as disturbing to their time as these new mendicants are on the byways of the new world. They protest the emptiness and formalism of modern life, even as their predecessors cut through the formalities of conventional religion as they sought the reality of Christian existence and community.

If the "turned-off" generation were merely an extremist sect which had no relations to the new generation, we might find it interesting for research but not terribly relevant for comprehending the new society. However, this new mendicancy, like its forebears, brings to focus the anxieties and aspirations of a whole generation. It develops these aspirations with sectarian fervor. It isolates itself by intensity but it gives focus to its generation, radicalizing the search of the new generation. It acts and speaks *for* the rebellious generation. Its power to move the youth of today gives the new mendicancy its significance and potential threat to the techno-culture.

The Woodstock Music and Art Festival in Bethel, New York, from August 15 to 17, 1969, drew over 300,000 young people to a six-hundred-acre farm for a communal gathering of rock music, drugs ànd communion. This gathering was not at all unique for the new generation, though it outdid previous festivals in numbers and organizational difficulties. The new generation shares the participatory consciousness which was considered in the first chapter. It senses its common world, but it lacks forms to shape that world. It shares music and mood, common enjoyment of drugs and the search for new subjective wholeness. It feels a sense of community and expresses it in congregating for festivals.

If the "turned-off" culture can be likened to the lay mendicancy of the waning middle ages, then the festivals of the new generation are comparable to the great holy days of medieval Catholicism. On those occasions the everyday life of the market and peasant hut came to intense expression in celebration. The unity of life found symbolic expression; the various parts of the medieval world were drawn together and renewed through the great symbols and festivals. For a brief moment men felt their common humanity, accepting once again their particular burdens and destinies. The fragmented life of everyday was restored in a momentary glimpse of eternity. The burdens of a particular fate were momentarily lightened by the transforming grace of a truer reality.

We do not mean to romanticize the Rock Festivals of the new generation nor to pass over some of the more chaotic events its exuberance has wrought on beaches and in little towns. Nor do we mean to pass over the difficulties and dangers inherent in its preoccupation with drugs. Nevertheless, we are witnessing a communal movement of national and even global scope. The participatory consciousness is accompanied by a profound search for a new sensibility. The festival gatherings are esthetic experiences. Whatever the vagaries into which this search may be thrown by the techno-culture which spawned it, a deep hunger for authentic personal existence and true community is moving the new generation. Radical sects like the "turned-off" culture give this search intensity—opening new possibilities. We might say, at the risk of pushing the analogy to medieval life a bit too far, that the new generation yearns for the Great Congregation; it seeks a human community—promised by a participatory consciousness but destroyed by the very technology which evoked it. The festival is earnest of this grace but lacks a continuing form. Where this will lead and what faith it may generate remain to be seen. In the festival at least there is a foretaste of the community to come and a renewal of hope. In the barren surroundings of the techno-culture, the wasteland is momentarily transformed by human sensibility and intimacy.

If one doubted that the Rock Festivals were an authentic challenge to the establishment, he would only have to read editorials and comment on the Woodstock Festival in an establishment newspaper like *The New York Times*. Its first editorial expressed the revulsion of the power structure at the search for community among the new generation. In an editorial, dated August 18, 1969, *The New York Times* referred to "maddened youths" and likened their mood to "the impulses that drive the lemmings to march to their deaths in the sea" (p. 20). Despite the vituperation which the *Times* heaped on the youth who attended the festival, partially modified in a subsequent editorial, it acknowledged grudgingly that the young people had conducted themselves with remarkable grace under unbelievably difficult conditions. The establishment finds it impossible to see and hear what is happening in this new generation because it lacks eyes and ears, and because the consciousness and aspirations of the rebellious generation reach beyond anything which the older generation can experience. This is the gap which makes the conflict between the generations so serious. The tragedy of techno-man is that he is programmed to receive only the feedback which his calculations have anticipated.

To speak of the new mendicancy of the "turned-off" culture, and of an authentic "religious celebration," is not to affirm either form unequivocally. Religious expressions are notoriously ambiguous. They contain demonic as well as divine qualities. We have already observed some weaknesses in the "turned-off" culture; indeed, its privatization of protest in fantasy and drugs means that its power to challenge the techno-culture is extremely limited. Similar reservations can be adduced against important trends in the new esthetic and communal congregating of the rebellious generation. The spontaneity is too often an undisciplined expression of feeling which gains little continuing space in the world. The dependence on drugs is not much more promising than the dependence of the establishment on alcohol and tranquillizers. And the mass congregating, however exhilarating as the momentary experience, lacks day-to-day forms to shape a future. There is a demonic immediacy in the new esthetic which will disillusion its adherents, leaving them even more vulnerable to the lures of the technically competent society and undermining their search for an authentic human style.

The new esthetic and communalism reach for a radically different manhood from the Protestant image of the Western tradition. Whatever its weaknesses, then, this is the important disclosure of the "turned-off" culture. They reject the promise of increased control which the technologists dream of effecting through computers, genetics and chemicals. The new generation seeks an existential revolution which reaches beyond the sterile rationality of technical competence. It is experimenting with feeling and sensibility in order to arrive at some wholeness of body, mind and spirit which can realize true humanness. It is living in a sexual openness which can break through disembodied rationality. It is searching out communion and intimacy in order to break through the objectification of man. In brief, it is struggling for personal, human, whole, embodied existence. It is struggling for soul, for being human in a world which has made everything into a calculable object of domination. It is searching for belonging and participation over against making and controlling.

CONFLICT BETWEEN THE GENERATIONS

THE STRUGGLE BETWEEN generations is certainly as old as man. Whatever the form of the society, parents are obliged to maintain the accepted standards of behavior. This vested obligation of older people inevitably conflicts with the innovative spirit of the young. It is the nature of youth to try the untried and reach for the not yet known. This dynamic of youth gives societies a creative thrust which only the most traditionalized forms can restrain. In most societies those traditional forms are closely intertwined with parental and ancestral authorities. To innovate is often to contradict the authority of the elders, yet the elders too look hopefully for that innovation as a creativity which they cherish yet are obliged to restrain.

A strange paradox of high technology societies is the intense conflict between generations even when the elders are committed to innovation. Technology by its nature institutionalizes innovation as a way of life. The more efficient means is automatically taken to be better. This is a distinctive mark of high technology societies and accounts for much of the dislocation which they cause. Controlling groups invest their careers in readiness to innovate at almost any cost. John McDermott speaks of this basic principle of technological societies as *laissez innover*, linking the newer society to the interests of the free market.

Why should the new generation rebel against its parents and other authorities in a society which encourages innovation? How, indeed, is one to comprehend the rebellion of the new generation against a society made to order for its vitalities?

This paradox deepens when one ponders the removal of parental authority as a significant factor in high technology societies. The parents, after all, are not a very serious restraint upon the actions and interests of older young people. Conservative adults mutter in dismay at some of the activities of young people in their festival gatherings. They look askance at parents whom they expect to discipline these young people. Even university administrators have turned desperately to parents in hopes of gaining additional disciplinary leverage on students. Needless to say, these efforts have proved futile. Parents do not exercise this kind of authority in a high technology society, or at least parents of middle- and upper-middle-class children no longer exercise such an authoritative role.

The reduction of parental authority is functional in high technology societies, because sciences and techniques are constantly changing and draw very little on the more traditional understandings passed on from parents to children. Excessive parental authority is a handicap in a techno-culture. Hence, parents see their children educated out of their hands at an early age. Much like immigrant parents, they see their children entering a new world which will always be a bit strange to them.

In many ways, conflict between the generations should be rather mitigated in the American situation. The American techno-culture encourages innovation. It also shifts much of the weight of parental authority to peer groups, schools and media. Nevertheless, the conflict between generations appears to be exacerbated year by year. Seldom have parents been so concerned for their children; rarely if ever have children so radically challenged their parents' values. Hence, there would seem to be a much deeper basis of conflict between the generations than meets the eye. This is more than a matter of conservative elders restraining the innovative spirit of the young. It is more than a struggle over parental authority. The conflict between generations seems to arise from the deeper struggle against the principle of control which directs the techno-culture.

The suggestion of a deeper conflict finds some support in the rioting at the Democratic Convention in Chicago in the summer of 1968. The convention was the scene of a head-on collision between established authority and the new generation. This was a tragic but extremely revealing confrontation and merits reflection.

Much has been said and written about the Police Riot at the Democratic Convention in Chicago. Little is to be gained from rehearsing the nightmare which was so well depicted in the Walker Report. But one theme stands out through all the events of that shocking week: the young people were impatient with public authority, while the established powers were determined to control these young people. This was an open confrontation with authority. The peace groups coming to Chicago in protest against President Johnson's Vietnam policy were not necessarily out to oppose every vestige of public authority, but they were certainly ready for a confrontation by the time Mayor Daley had refused them living space and rights to demonstrate. However, the peace groups were from the start augmented by many sympathetic though unschooled young people. The Police Riot mobilized many young people on the side of the peace groups. In the battle of Chicago, young people discovered that public authority was not only against them but would terrorize them if it could not control them. Moreover, young people began to express their opposition to control by the establishment and particularly in the person of its principal arm—the police. Mayor Daley and his police were then arrayed against the peace groups and thousands of sympathetic young people. The battle lines were drawn and open conflict ensued.

We are not concerned here to justify the actions of either side, although the Walker Report made it quite clear that the fault lay heavily on the side of the public authorities. The striking fact is that many American parents sympathized with the police in their treatment of the young people. Furthermore, the young people almost without exception were aligned with their peers against established authority; indeed, a large number of young people were radicalized by this confrontation. The battle of the Chicago Convention thus brings to light a deep struggle for control which is far more general in the society than most of us are willing to acknowledge.

We have seen many repetitions of this struggle on university campuses and in peace marches—most dramatically perhaps in the beatings administered to young people by marshals and troops in the March on the Pentagon. We do well to reflect very deeply on these events. The central reality in the confrontations is the new generation's unwillingness to bow to established authority. It feels constrained and controlled. The society may honor innovation and creativity, yet it insists on setting the terms for that innovation and controlling access to opportunity by imposing long periods of training. This permissive society with its reduced parental authority is actually extremely authoritative about controlling its young people. Instead of coping with parental authority until puberty and then managing to live with parents and elders in intimate relationships for a lifetime, our young people now pass rather quickly under the tutelage of peer groups, extended schooling and bureaucratized organizations. They see no escape from the invisible controls of the techno-culture. They speak of this as "getting caught in the system."

The invisible authority of the techno-culture dominates the new generation with faceless violence. The police give personal expression to this authority, but they represent an authority which they do not originate or control. The police represent "law and order," but whose "law" and whose "order" are not discussable. The answers to questions like these are a bash in the face and a knee in the groin. The violence against the new generation expresses the deep commitment of the techno-culture to control its young people. The liberal attitudes and permissive homes are a façade for repressive control. Young people have not spearheaded opposition to the American system in previous periods. Revolts by the American Indian tribes, by slaves on plantations, by ethnic groups and industrial workers and more recently by rural workers have been suppressed with violence. This has been the pattern in the emerging American way of life. But now we are seeing the same principle at work on the new generation. And well might the Black people of Chicago have reflected on the first time Whites were on the receiving end. This was the irony of the Chicago Convention. Whites of the establishment were beating their own. The techno-culture had reached the ultimate in self-contradiction.

The protests of the "turned-off" generation are at least unconsciously directed at the invisible controls of the techno-culture. The knife turns in the establishment's belly when young people appear with long hair, bare feet, painted faces, naked, using obscene language and crying "Pig." These are countermeasures to the exquisite internal control which middle-class families have imposed on these young people. The new generation is provoking the older generation to show its hand—to come into the open with the coercive control which it has exercised from the start. This hand was shown in the Police Riot at the Convention, 1968. Moreover, there was little pressure for discipline of the offending police except from the Walker Report and the American Civil Liberties Union. The matter was quickly dropped.

The conflict between generations is intense within the

techno-culture because controls are invisible and all-encompassing. The crisis in the universities comes into perspective when we perceive the crucial role of higher education in imprinting the American way on the younger generation. Universities operate by rational discussion. So far so good, since classrooms are places where books are interpreted and ideas discussed. Students realize that their future prospects depend upon their achievements in the academic system. They know that the standards for achievement, content of programs and judgments of competence are set by the faculties. Students also find that their protests over the quality of their education and the careerist preoccupation of their professors go unheard, as the Cox Report on the Columbia University confrontation made clear. In brief, coercive power over the lives and hopes of students is now vested in institutions of higher education. These institutions are managed by trustees, administrators and faculties. They exercise invisible control over the life chances of the young. When their control is challenged by student sit-ins and demonstrations, educational authorities protest that they have no power. They rule by rational discussion.

This picture of the campus conflict is, of course, rather one-sided, since it is drawn to illumine the centrality of the problem of control in our techno-culture. Whatever questions one may raise about the tactics used by students in the confrontations, the coercive character of higher education is such that this is a head-on power struggle over who is to control the future of the new generation. This means that the confrontation will sooner or later come to rest in the faculty-student relationship, because faculty members hold the power of vocational life and death over their students in the new society.

The real difficulty with the student protest is not its tactics, though these have often been barbarous and ineffective. Their real difficulty is that they are caught in the vicious circle of coercion which surrounds a technological order. In struggling for a voice in the university power structure, students are caught in the same vicious circle which now traps faculty and administration. The problem of the university is not *who* controls it but *what* education means. Education, now, reflects the techno-culture. Getting a voice in the educational system means nothing unless the real significance of education is clearly understood. The question is not who has power in the university, but what the university is doing. This is the question that neither faculty nor administrators have been able to discuss—rationally or otherwise. They have their careers. Some have lucrative ties with industrial-military-governmental networks. They do not wish to be bothered, and unhappily this is true of many students as well. It may seem strange, but faculty and students have turned each confrontation into a power struggle, avoiding the real issue of what it means to educate and be educated.

Higher education today faces crisis of soul and truth. For the most part, the conflict between the controlling culture and the search for soul is blunted and obscured in the campus revolt. The crisis of soul is the heart of the university question and cannot be resolved in a struggle for power.

The struggle on the campuses defines the crisis as a power struggle, and there is no doubt that a more equitable distribution of power is desirable. Sympathies with campus protest arise in the student body, however, from frustration over the irrelevance of much academic work to problems of human existence. Students sense that they are not being educated. This is the underlying issue in the campus revolt. When preoccupation with control gives way to serious reflection on what it means to be a whole person and what, if anything, education has to do with becoming human and shaping a good society, then faculties and students may transcend the impasse in which techno-education has trapped them. They may begin to discuss authentic education together and find a new pedagogy.

We are proposing, then, that the techno-culture cherishes innovation on its own terms. It accepts feedback but not authentic dialogue. By its nature such a society casts a network of controls over existence, programming the minds and futures of its youth. Consequently, the innovations which it encourages only reinforce the system. Innovations in thought, politics and fundamental issues are taboo and will be suppressed with violence when they appear. So the vaunted innovation of the techno-culture occurs only within the narrow confines of its own programs. Challenges to the educational venture itself will simply not be tolerated. They bring into question the ground on which the techno-culture rests; that is, they question the premise that the system possesses the truth and loyalty to the system is equivalent to pursuit of truth.

Here, however, the crisis of soul discloses its tragic character. Protests within the techno-culture lack ground from which to challenge the system. We have already seen this tragic impasse in the campus revolt which devolves into a power struggle between faculty and students over control of a process that really obstructs instead of furthering education. The problem is not who controls but the single and sovereign principle of control itself. If control is the meaning of human existence and the ultimate criterion of truth—understanding, prediction and control—then techno-man holds all the cards. This is the radical question in the probing, searching, exploring and exploding struggle of the new generation. It is the question which is gnawing at the vitals of the whole American system. And this is the question which baffles the established generation as it tries to understand the crisis that grips the young. The older generation is so committed to control as the meaning of existence, including its own invisible control over the coming generation, that it cannot comprehend the groaning, painful search by the new generation to find a humanity beyond control and productivity. Its only resource for responding to the revolt of youth is its inner malaise, which creates a certain sympathy. Of course, the deeper reality here is that a life devoted to controlling reality comes up hard against the uncontrollable in oneself, in others and in the universe.

The struggle against control by the new generation sheds light on the problem of drugs in American society. Drugs, and by this we mean primarily the hallucinogens which are appealing to middle- and upper-class youth, create anxiety in the older generation. To be sure, there are "bad trips" and some realistic fears can be harbored against such drugs, particularly in their long-term effects. However, drugs reveal a distance between the older and newer generation which underlines the peculiar, new kind of struggle for soul that engages American society in this period. LSD and other hallucinogens are ways of releasing control over oneself, submitting to powers beyond one's calculations and previous training. These drugs break the controls so carefully contrived by parents and social institutions. They break the invisible hold of the society. Hence, these drugs run directly counter to the whole meaning of existence on which the older generation has built its world. They represent the breaking up of the rule of will, calculation and control which is the latter-day version of the Protestant ethic. The very idea of such drugs is not only abhorrent to the older generation, it is actually beyond its comprehension. These drugs explode the techno-culture.

We have been arguing that the crisis of soul arises from the impoverished psyche of techno-man. We have stressed the opening up of a life of feeling and community over against objective rationality and depersonalized existence. If existence is open to feeling, depth, awe and mystery—the incalculable as well as calculable—then control cannot be the single and sovereign principle of existence. There must be depths and inner reaches of experience and truth which extend beyond the controllable. Truth is far more encompassing than measurable effects. And techno-man is a partial, very limited perspective on a rich, encompassing world. The new generation seizes upon hallucinogenic drugs as a way of exploring this encompassing reality—as a way of shedding the controls of techno-man. Mind-expanding and mind-exploding experiences break the invisible controls. In a world constituted by and for control, drugs appear as countercultural —the rejection of control. Where alcohol sedates the controlling will, drugs open the will to the uncontrollable. Drugs symbolize and mediate the new generation's struggle for soul as a radical break with the calculable world of techno-man.

Deliverance from domination by techno-culture will take more than festivals, confrontations and drugs. Mind-expanding drugs may give some earnest of such release, but evidence indicates that this is an evanescent liberation. Drugs disclose both the search for soul and the powerlessness of the new generation. After all, the techno-culture is far more advanced and skilled in the administration of drugs than its young rebels; indeed, the turn toward drugs reflects dependence upon technology. If the battle is to be waged on this front, there is no question who will emerge as victor. The established order is already maintaining itself through ingestions of alcohol and tranquillizers. It can easily develop drugs to adjust the rebellious youth.

The real issue is how one deals with the undergirding reality of the techno-society—really coping with its principle of control. This means finding a way to transcend the principle of control, including control of one's psyche with drugs. "Dropping out" and "tripping out" are kinds of transcendence. Violent confrontations are also a mode of transcendence, since they create distance through negation. But negation can do little more than open a space for challenging the technological drive to make everything a means to productivity. That challenge has to draw upon an alternative reality which is more promising for humanity than the rule of the productive system. The negation is trying to get around technology by technical means. The problem is how to get through and beyond technology so that it can serve man rather than control him.

BEYOND TECHNO-MAN

THE CRISIS OF "soul" deepens the understanding of the struggle for freedom in high technology societies. It illumines the cultural crisis of the meaning of human existence in the productive system. We find a yearning for wholeness and sensibility which is turning the new generation against the system. The new generation is reaching for a psychic freedom beyond the systems of control which have been devised by the productive system. There is an authentic ground for this search, because freedom is more than participation in the consumer society, it is more than having a voice in the system. Being free is finding fulfillment in the realization of one's possibilities for joy, wonder, human intimacy and grace, as well as for productive activity.

We seem at times to be saying that the productive system is a new devil in a modern cosmology, but this is only because we have looked at the crisis of "soul" from the perspective of the new generation, who feel crushed by this oppressive system. Many young people do seem

bent upon bringing all of these institutions down around
them. Others seem disillusioned even with the protest;
they are resigned to finding solace in drugs and "counter-
cultures." But the rational ordering of things in service to
man's productive will is no devil—it is a healthy aspect of
man's freedom to shape and order his world. It only
becomes demonic when it takes possession of man. When
man becomes possessed by the producer–consumer syndrome—the productive will—his existence is impoverished, his sensibilities deadened and his public world
becomes an instrument of further control. When all things
become means to further domination, whether in free
enterprise systems or in collectivist states, then man
loses his soul; and to lose one's soul is to lose nature,
other people and finally one's humanity. So it is the
goodness and creativity of man's productive will that now
possesses and destroys him. It is against this demonic
possession that the new generation is rebelling.

We have generalized unabashedly about the new generation but only to lift out certain themes running through
the protests of our time. There is obviously no single new
generation. Even the "turned-off" young people present a
multiplicity of styles of life. The drug culture subsumes
not one philosophy but many. We turned attention earlier
to the hallucinogenic drugs; marijuana and speed have
different—though not unrelated—effects. We recognize
the selectivity of any interpretation which we impose
upon such a chaotic scene, and so we have to speak with
reservation in discussing a crisis of "soul." Yet it is clear
that a new challenge is being raised to the productive
system—a challenge that in its different manifestations
seems to well up from a fundamental source—the profound yearning for wholeness and human sensibility. The
clue to understanding this source is to be found in the
bearer of the search for a new cultural style: the younger
generation of the establishment. The turn toward inwardness, intimacy and sensibility among the establishment

rebels gives reason to believe that the crisis of "soul" is endemic to the productive culture.

The turn to inwardness demonstrates the depth of the crisis and at the same time betrays the weakness of the response in the new generation. Preoccupation with inwardness is the traditional focus of religious search in the American experience. Thus the "turning-off" and "turning-on" in the new generation are part and parcel of American pietism, though we have probably not had such drug-induced pietism in earlier periods. The new note in this contemporary pietism is its rebellion against the productive system. The older forms encouraged a virtuous and productive life. The productive system can tolerate inwardness so long as it does not directly threaten the working of the system. Indeed, as automation reduces opportunities for active engagement in the productive processes, it may be desirable to retire large numbers of the new generation to harmless personal and communal preoccupations. In a short time the rebel culture could become the dependent culture, and the oppressive system would continue to hold sway. To this extent, the New Left are far more reality-minded even if less radical in their questioning of the techno-culture. They realize that the system has to be challenged on an objective ground, though they have yet to discern and disclose that ground.

Hence, the subjective crisis of "soul" brings us to the deeper question of an objective ground upon which the technological system can be challenged and transcended. That ground lies within our Western heritage, but it is concealed by the triumph of productivity over all of man's other possibilities. The virtue of the protesting generation is its refusal to accept concealment of the democratic heritage any longer. They are making it perfectly clear that the American dream of a free society and the American hope for a free world are being destroyed by America itself. This brings us, then, to the objective, cultural crisis which now besets American democracy.

CHAPTER IV

Toward Cultural Revolution

REVOLUTION MEANS RADICAL change in thought or political structure. We speak of the Copernican Revolution, through which our geocentric understanding in astronomy was overthrown; we speak of the French Revolution, in which both the form of government and the composition of the ruling class were changed. Obviously, a "cultural revolution" is closer to a revolution in thought than in form of government. But a cultural revolution is more extensive and fundamental than a radical change in a system of thought. Revolutionary change in culture means radical questioning of the principles which shape and order the common life. Such a revolution affects thought in a society, but it also brings into question the grounds upon which a particular system—in this case the productive system of technology—dominates and organizes man's world.

Social critics divide into two broad groups over the question of social change today. The larger group are of the opinion that the Western technological system will prevail in the world, probably moving toward a modified state socialism yet preserving many liberties of the democratic heritage. We could call this the reformist group, recognizing many shades of opinion among its members, all the way from those who opt for an automatic, market system to those who believe a considerable amount of regulation is necessary. The other, revolutionary, group also represents a wide variety of opinions on our present situation and its possibilities. The majority of the revolutionary group look to a traditional type of revolution to bring about radical collectivism in the organization of society and to make the benefits of technology available to all. The political revolutionaries today are drawn toward a Third World coalition, since they recognize that objective conditions for a radical revolution do not seem to exist within the high technology societies.

To speak of cultural revolution is to break with both reformists and political revolutionaries. It is to question the possibility of human fulfillment under the conditions of a technological order, whether that order is dominated by an Overclass of managers in a democratic tradition or a revolutionary elite in a Maoist tradition. If one opts for cultural revolution he is questioning the premises of the Western development and especially the principle that productivity and unlimited growth can lead to human fulfillment.

On matters like reform or revolution, one has to distinguish between judgments as to what is the case and what would be desirable goals. Judgments of fact and value

shade into one another among social critics when they
discuss possible changes in social institutions during the
next decades of world history. It is not so easy to distinguish the reforms one hopes to see from the actual reforms which may occur in the years to come. And to title
a chapter "Toward Cultural Revolution" is to build the
ambiguity between fact and value into one's reflections.
This could mean encouragement to think and act toward
a radical change in the principles which now control
Western development. It could also mean that we are
moving in this direction and can best carry out our reflections by using this context to clarify what we are experiencing. The latter perspective guides our analysis.

The theme "Toward Cultural Revolution" is used here
to express the empirical judgment that we are moving
into a revolutionary situation. Moreover, the basic principles which have shaped Western development and led to
the West's colonial expansion over the globe are now
coming into question. The revolutionary challenge may
come through reforms and/or by means of change in the
power structures which manage the system. But the
deeper challenges within these upheavals are addressed to
the technological system itself as a way of life. Whether
these challenges will lead to fundamental changes in our
system is another question. They may be suppressed, but
they cannot be ignored.

The technological order of life is rapidly becoming a
worldwide system. It emerged in Europe, reached its
zenith in the American system and is now extending its
sway over the globe. We shall consider challenges to the
system in the American experience, but we do so in full
recognition that comparable negations are appearing in
all parts of the world. The American experience is particularly illuminating because it is far and away the most
advanced in its unqualified institutionalization of a technological order of life. At the same time, the United
States of America has a peculiar history and particular

cultural traditions which make it as unique in global history as the Japanese experience. We can probably generalize somewhat from the American case if we are cautious and recognize certain cultural limitations in this experience. The transcultural, universal character of the technological order, more than anything else, makes global comparisons possible and useful.

Four basic challenges to the American system have emerged in recent decades. Two of these are internal to the system and two are external. The internal challenges are the revolt of the new generation and the new visibility of the Black community. We have already explored aspects of these internal negations of the American system; in the following section we will deepen our reflections on the challenge of the Black experience. The external negations are the threatened breakdown of the environmental life support systems and the defeat of American military strategy in the Vietnam stalemate. The challenge of the environment may prove to be the most threatening negation of the basic premises of the technological order. What Paul Ehrlich has called our emerging "eco-catastrophe" may prove the turning point in the cultural revolution. There is no indication that this problem can be handled without contravening the principles of the technological order. In the following pages we shall focus attention on the Vietnam experience, because its immediate impact is more evident and its implications for our global situation relatively clear.

If the cultural revolution were maturing, new styles of life and thought would be in evidence. Qualities such as sensitivity and imagination would become more prominent among political and intellectual leaders. Our heritage of democratic rights would transform institutional racism and lead to serious action on problems of poverty. Our confessional heritage would motivate new moral commitment and communal forms. But the time is not ripe. At the most, we are experiencing exploratory stirrings of the

new age. Our civil and confessional heritages are so
completely assimilated to the technological system that
they no longer furnish distance and self-criticism. We
suffer from a collapse of transcendence, and so challenges
to the system have to arise over against our tradition. The
polarizations which we now experience in American life
are only symptomatic of this inner and outer negation of
the American system.

The collapse of transcendence sets the stage for our
reflection on the internal and external challenges to the
American way of life. By "transcendence" here we mean
the distance from ourselves which we gain by seeing
ourselves through another person or culture or movement.
We only gain such transcendence through another person
or event when we realize that we cannot possess, control
or dominate this reality. So long as we can impose our
stereotypes on other groups, fitting them to images which
categorize them and prevent us from seeing ourselves as
they see us, we protect ourselves from the transcendence
which they could bring to us—from the judgment on our
exploitative attitudes and greed. But rejecting such transcendence through the other person or group costs us a
great deal of energy, because we share in their lives and
meanings on the deeper levels of our experience and have
to suppress those shared feelings in order to defend ourselves from them and their needs. This is the peculiar
duality of human existence. We are distant from others,
ultimately alone in our consciousness and dependent on
communication to hear and know one another. At the
same time, we are united with others; we share meanings,
symbols, feelings and embodied life and thus we belong
together in the world and need to bring our shared world
to expression as community of shared concern. So there is
a uniqueness and particularity to each person, group and
culture which can never be assimilated to a category or
system, and there is also a shared, common world of
meanings, feelings and embodiment which each person,

group and culture draws upon to understand others and to communicate its own uniqueness.

If we absolutize our uniqueness and the way in which we have embodied the shared meanings of humanness, then we refuse to hear and see the meanings which others express. We enclose ourselves in our own systems, cut ourselves off from the enlarging human community to which our existence is called and confine ourselves to the limitations of our own stereotypes. When this happens, other persons, groups and cultures challenge us either in their refusal to submit to our stereotypes and domination or in an open attack upon our system of control.

We are at a point in Western development where the American technological system has closed off the resources of transcendence from its own heritage. This is what we mean by a collapse of transcendence. However, internal and external challenges are being thrown up against this system as negations or transcendent judgments. If these judgments are responded to creatively, they may be modes of recovering our civic and confessional heritages, because they will disclose the exploitative character of the techno-culture and reveal the true promise of our heritage.

Two Challenges to the American System

In Chapter ii the Black struggle was conceived as forerunner of the struggle of the Underclass for a voice. However, that reflection merely touched the surface of the Black struggle in America. We now have to press our

considerations to the cultural level on which fundamental
questions about the American enterprise come into view.
The visibility of the Black man in America is one locus of
such fundamental questioning. In that framework we reopen our reflections on the Black struggle.

We owe the notion of "Black visibility" to Charles
Long. He drew attention to this dimension of transcendence in a landmark essay which has been too little discussed: "The Black Reality: Toward a Theology of Freedom." In this essay Mr. Long made note of otherness of
the Black experience in White America. That otherness
confronts White America. The Rights Movement and separatist struggles bring the Black man into view. The
instinctive response of White techno-man is to do something about the Blacks. He wants to assert his control by
integrating Blacks or adjusting them or appeasing them
or whatever. The genius of techno-man is that he can
manage things, yet here is the unmanageable Black loom-
ing on his horizon and discomfiting him. What can he do?

We take our point of departure from Charles Long's
insight into this confrontation between Black and White
America. We want to plumb some of the depths of this
meeting with the otherness of the Black man. However,
we take a somewhat different line of reflection from Mr.
Long's. We are, for one thing, trying to grasp this situation from within the White experience and especially
from within the techno-culture. If our basic notion of
two-way communication in Chapter II is sound, it is essential that both Blacks and Whites take the time and
effort to illumine this confrontation from their own
perspectives. It is obvious that Whites have defined the
Black situation for too many years. Black intellectuals
leaders and artists are rapidly correcting those White
perspectives, but the Black definition can distort the situation in the opposite direction unless we achieve some
interchange of perspectives. Charles Long's paper opens

the consideration of freedom on the deepest level. We shall try to look at the other side of the coin. We want to consider control and domination—the will of techno-man —to grasp the peculiar depths of racism in the American experience. We believe that we can find its roots in the technological will. This will-to-power is brought into question in the meeting with Black otherness. Black visibility brings judgment to White America, disclosing the limitations and distortions of the all-encompassing technological will.

The uncontrollable otherness of the Black Movement emerged slowly in the last decades. At first the Rights Movement leaned heavily on federal authority against local customs, seeking to extend fundamental rights of citizenship. This struggle came to a turning point on the Meredith March in Mississippi when Black Power became a rallying cry for the new generation of Blacks. From that point onward the Afro-American theme has become more and more prominent. The links between Black America and its African heritage have preoccupied Black students. The Black Panthers brought this Black consciousness into the streets of the ghettos, mobilizing Black political consciousness. In less than a decade the Black struggle for rights became a Black assertion of communal independence as Black people. This was a startlingly rapid transition from an attempt to "make it" in the White system to a determination to "make it" on Black terms.

White liberals and even the techno-planners could understand and deal with the Black struggle for rights. The key to the human rights movement is the notion that race, religion and ethnic origin are not relevant criteria for discriminating among individuals or groups. The techno-culture is built on criteria of competence and performance, so that any other criteria of inclusion or exclusion are limiting to the system. Hence, the White Overclass could basically affirm a Black Movement which hoped to throw off old restraints and enter fully into the system. White techno-man could welcome Blacks into the system on White terms, but Black Power struck a discordant note. Black separatism and Afro-Americanism are ways of saying "Color is important!" The Black Movement was asserting that Blackness was inextricably woven into a Black future.

Black separatism disclosed a profound ambivalence in the Black Movement. Since political power and economic resources were vested in White America, the Black Movement had to find some means of drawing on those resources in order to develop Black America. At the same time, White America kept control over those whom it funded whether through domestic or foreign aid. If the Black colony in America turned to White America for resources, was it not strengthening the controls of the White Overclass over Black people? On the other hand, a participatory society requires a broad floor of technological resources for minimal participation, so Black communities urgently needed economic and social development if they were not to be permanently fixed as a dependent Underclass. Here then emerged the inescapable ambivalence of Black separatism in a participatory society—dependence on resources and a drive for Black independence.

This ambivalence came to striking expression in James Forman's Black Manifesto to Churches and other agencies for reparations to be paid to the Black Economic Development Conference (see Appendix 1). Most of the laity in the Churches appear to have been generally opposed to the demand for reparations. Even the liberal religious leadership have been extremely uncertain, and many of them have tried to discount the Preamble to the Manifesto with the view to acknowledging the justice of the demand for reparations. The important fact about the Manifesto, however, is that the demand for reparations—for justice —is coupled with the Preamble in which White America is condemned and rejected. The resources of White technology are useful and acceptable—even owed to the Black man—so long as the Black ethos determines their use and significance for Black development.

The Black Movement is extremely complex. It includes such diverse strands as Operation Breadbasket, which is developing Black Capitalism as a base for Black Power, and the Student National Coordinating Committee, which has dispensed with its "non-violent" tradition and now attacks the whole system of White America as enslaving to Black people. The enormous variety in the Black Movement would be obscured and distorted if we tried to encapsulate its themes in a single confrontation like the Black Manifesto. Nevertheless, fundamental motifs in the confrontation of Black and White America come together in the Manifesto, taken seriously in both the Preamble and the demand for reparations. The Preamble rejects White control and domination. Rejecting the future of White America, it sees a future in a wholly different social organization, stressing collective, communal values, which will make possible a Black America connected with the Third World. We are not so much concerned here with the Third World motif, though that dimension lifts up the unity with Africa which is crucial to Black identity, but rather with the basic rejection of the White techno-culture and its Overclass and the sense of a Black future which can only emerge from Black identity, Black self-respect and Black organization.

Black reality, then, confronts White America and its techno-culture with a basic challenge. White liberals have been trying to use the Black Movement in order to achieve White purposes in social and political goals of the liberal movements. Now the Black Movement is rejecting the White agenda out of hand. White urbanologists who hoped to appease ghetto Blacks with token programs in order to free planners and bureaucrats to go ahead with development of systems for White America, and especially for White suburbia, are running head-on into a recalcitrant Black Movement which refuses to be appeased or organized or bought.

The rank and file of the Black community could probbly be bought off, just as White communities are constantly bought off by political machines. But the leadership of the Black community is increasingly aware that there is a fundamental contradiction between White America and an authentic Black future. Whether Black leadership can sustain this prophetic insight and maintain its position against the lures of the White techno-culture is not our immediate concern, though it will certainly be extremely difficult to carry through this position without success in obtaining development resources. Nevertheless, Black leadership and visibility challenge the whole system of White control and thus confront the basic principle of the techno-culture. By demanding a share of the wealth—some of which was originally capitalized in slave traffic—the Black Movement is acknowledging the network of interdependence which technology generates. In rejecting White America, the Black Movement is denying any possibility of assimilating Black identity and the Black future to White America on White terms.

Let us go a step beyond this Black Manifesto and make an interpretation of the ground for the rejection of White America. Subjected from the first to control by White America, the Black community rebelled against second-class citizenship, and now challenges the future of White America. Rejecting the White will-to-domination which seeks to organize a Black future as well as a global hegemony, Black people are opting for independent development.

And the Black Movement is on good ground in rejecting

this White will-to-domination, which was the source of Black enslavement and is also the root of American racism.

When one reflects in a broad historical context, racism in White America is a puzzling phenomenon. Only South Africa begins to parallel it. Various studies of racial prejudice have adduced many, but rather unconvincing, reasons for this racism. Even Gordon Allport, who devoted years of research to the problem, ended up by clustering factors and levels of prejudice which seem to merge in America's racist syndrome. We propose here, by contrast, that American racism is grounded in the obedient will of our Protestant heritage. The Black man was excluded from participation in the promise of a free, obedient people at the outset. The Black man was from the first the antithesis of White obedience. He was the non-person, the non-will. He was from the first the contradiction to the unlimited sway of God over nature and history through White obedience.

Bonded White servants who were brought to these shores could and did work their way out of indebtedness. There were fortunates and unfortunates who landed on these shores. There were privileged and deprived. Yet the New World offered opportunities to break out of social and legal bonds. Gradually opportunities opened beyond anything earlier settlers might have imagined. Openness, freedom and opportunity became dominant motifs.

The Black was the contradiction to this development, the antithesis to the promise of this New World. The White will-to-power grew and expanded. From a desire to explore and settle, the White man was carried away by the dream of mastery. Meanwhile, the Black man was held in subservience. The White man saw himself as a child of promise in a blessed land. Day by day he schooled the Blacks as children of bondage. The White man saw himself as the obedient servant of a beneficent Lord. He defined the Black as disobedient and soulless. The Black, then, was from the first an alien element in this land, a counter-reality to this venture in liberty and a living antithesis to the White will-to-power. The White found himself caught in the contradiction of denying will, rights, soul and humanity to this Black with whom he fornicated and labored. By simply leaving the Black out of the charter, the Constitution crystallized the contradiction. The Civil War brought to tragic disclosure the contradiction which the Emancipation Proclamation tried to resolve.

With the Civil War and its aftermath in Reconstruction and Jim Crow, the damage was done, and White will-to-power had become American reality. Blackness had become the antithesis—the anti-Puritanism, the unfree, the closed in, the powerless! Blacks had become all the things which Whites feared, including their own passions and feelings. Blacks had become the underside of the White will-to-power—the abyss of powerlessness.

America's religious heritage was gradually transformed into a will-to-power. From mastery over natural enemies and human vicissitudes the obedient will was slowly transmuted to the productive exploitative will. This White will projected upon the Black all of the passions and needs which were being suppressed in the struggle for control of the self and the world, acting out the hidden passions in miscegenation, rape and lynch. The evil, disobedient will which the guilt-ridden White dreaded was extruded from White consciousness and projected on the Black man. White America whipped itself ever more furiously in its passion to gain control of its environment, suppressing its life of feeling and oppressing immigrant groups who arrived to share the struggle. Thus the White techno-will emerged by stages and transmutations from the obedient will of a Puritan heritage to the exploitative will of the technological order. At each step of the way the Black man became bearer of the burden of disobedience, uncon-

trolled passion and exploitation which the White man hid
from his sight. Black became a symbol of the evil, incalculable and alien which the White man feared in himself.
The conscience of White techno-man was freed from guilt
and the stage was set for an infinite drive to master the
world.

Lillian Smith expressed the inner contradiction between
White obedience to God and suppression of truth in a
passage of *Killers of the Dream*. She was depicting the
roots of the racism in southern life. We find here the
contradiction in the White will-to-power which Blackness
symbolizes:

> *What a strange ugly trap the White race made for itself!
> Because these slaveholders were "Christian," they felt com-
> pelled to justify the holding of slaves by denying these
> slaves a soul, and denying them a place in the human fam-
> ily. Because they were puritan, they succeeded in develop-
> ing a frigidity in their white women that precluded the
> possibility of mutual satisfaction. Lonely and baffled and
> frustrated by the state of affairs they had set up in their
> own homes and hearts, they could not resist the vigor and
> kindliness and gaiety of these slaves. And succumbing to
> desire, they mated with these dark women whom they had
> dehumanized in their minds, and fathered by them children
> who, according to their race philosophy, were "without
> souls"—a strange exotic new kind of creature, whom they
> made slaves of and sometimes sold on the auction block.
> The white man's roles as slaveholder and Christian and
> puritan were exacting far more than the strength of his
> mind could sustain. Each time he found the back-yard
> temptation irresistible, his conscience split more deeply
> from his acts and his mind from things as they are* [p. 103].

The will-to-power, acted out against the Black and ration-
alized in denying him will and power, came to fruition in
America's techno-culture—subordinating every reality to

human mastery, each step of the way denying soul to others until White soul atrophied and White consciousness split. And now the contradiction in the will-to-power confronts White America in the progeny of those Black slaves. Here stands the last enemy of the will-to-power! Here is a people unwilling to surrender its soul. If Black people can be ground down to fit into the system, a completely technological, soulless urbanization is in reach and White will-to-power can impose itself upon all of reality, even obliterating the Blackness which its forebears had introduced. What wonder that the Black Movement sees surrender to the White American system as the final stage in its subjugation and the obliteration of a Black future.

We propose, then, that America's faith gradually became vested in the managerial will of domination and control. The obedient will of a Puritan heritage was transmuted to an unbounded will to control all of reality. How this occurred would be difficult to trace. We see it brilliantly portrayed by the picture which Lillian Smith drew in that classic volume, *Killers of the Dream*. Quite clearly Max Weber was depicting the emergence of man as productive, achieving, making and shaping will in the triumph of the Protestant ethic through Calvinism. Here the South African parallel is interesting: similar Calvinism and racism have characterized South African culture. Social scientists recognize the importance of this achievement drive in contemporary America. The "turned-off" generation is rebelling against this will-to-mastery, reaching out for esthetic sensibility and communal experience. The technological will-to-control emerging from our Puritan heritage as the obedient will under God became a commitment to unlimited growth and exploitation.

The Black man has from the outset been defined by the White as the antithesis to the obedient will; as the will-to-power gained ascendancy, Blackness became more and more alien and threatening. Charles Long's insight into the invisibility of the Black man for such a long period is helpful here. The Black man did not exist, because the only visible, existing man was the dominating will which could manage and control, and that managerial will was vested in White America. Those without control were non-existent—non-entities!

Black visibility confronts this debased Puritanism with an otherness which cannot be assimilated to White exploitation. Note the reactions in Church conventions to the Black Manifesto! All kinds of appeasement were suggested. Occasionally the justification of reparations was urged, but it was acted on only by the Episcopal Convention—September, 1969—and then through its own Black churchmen. In every case the managerial will was asserting itself. What shall we do? How shall we act? Where will we make the next move? There was little or no recognition that White America was under judgment nor that the whole American past was coming into question. There was no sense that America's religious faith was challenged, no acknowledgment that the whole American future was in doubt. Yet this is what the "turned-off" generation has been trying to say. And Black visibility is that profound, unavoidable challenge: White America has debased its faith and democratic heritage by an apotheosis of the White will-to-power.

Here, then, in Black visibility, the American system meets a transcendent judgment from within. At the heart of American urbanization arises a power which cannot be managed, controlled, put in its place, assimilated to the system. At least for the moment and under the impetus of powerful Black leadership, the Black man has become visible as the antithesis of White America. And what is to be done about it? That is the question which White history will have to unfold. What can be done now above all is to recognize that this is a real judgment. What can

and must be done if there is to be an American future is
to see the Black man. To recognize him! And in recognizing the Black man, to see White America. As Robert
Terry notes in *For Whites Only*, America is being challenged to a new White consciousness.

The revolt of the new generation has challenged the
impoverishment of man by the technological will. This
inward transcendence in White America points the way
toward a recovery of human wholeness and sensibility. It
is an existential revolt! Can we say anything about the
transcendence of Black visibility? What direction is
opened up with Black judgment? Does this encounter
point America to a possibility of transcending its debased
Protestant ethic? Is there grace in this judgment or only
the Day of Wrath?

One can read the confrontation of White and Black
America only with caution. Nevertheless, certain possibilities are beginning to emerge. Black otherness is borne by
a sizable Black population who now refuse to be submerged as an invisible Underclass. They are asserting a
claim to live out a Black possibility within the American
democracy. This possibility was refused to the Indian
cultures and later to Latin Americans. Now the refusal
puts White America in a serious crisis, because some of
the Black leadership insist on the possibility of being
Black and being American. So first of all, Black visibility
points toward cultural pluralism in the new, participatory
society. This is also the cry of the "turned-off" generation,
which is searching for a future outside the system. The
issue is whether there can be an open pluralistic techno-
culture. Can White America listen to Black America
with respect? Another aspect of the Black challenge is
elusive but significant. We noted America's tradition of
White violence which we can now comprehend as the
expression of the White will-to-power. Blacks have been
victims of that White violence throughout their American

experience. Whites and Blacks are entangled in a vicious
circle of violence from which there seems to be no exit.
Whites suppress Blacks through property controls, political machines, police brutality and, where necessary, military force. Blacks in turn look to weapons and force as a
way of retaliating or at least defending themselves. American militarism is only a last stage in this process. Black
visibility points beyond this tradition of violence in a
negative way. It embodies the limits of suppressive violence. The sheer survival of the Black is the counter-reality of White domination.

We gain a glimpse of the prophetic quality of Martin
Luther King, Jr. in opening this question of violence. He
has been accused of demanding that Black people bear a
witness of (non-violent) love which only further humili-
ated them before White Power. But his non-violent vision
had a deeper and more ultimate ground which still eludes
us. He sought the ground for humanization of all people.
Dr. King was pointing beyond domination, power and
violence to a reality in which White and Black peoples
could find redemption. He understood that Black reality
would be only a negation so long as it lived out of White
violence. He rejected that White debasement of its religious and democratic heritage. He envisioned a ground in
community and respect which transcended the vicious
circle of violence. We misunderstand this Black leader if
we read him simply as a tactician of the Black Movement
who happened to use non-violence. He had a dream of
human community beyond domination and violence, because he foresaw the doom of Black and White, and
indeed the whole creation was now entangled in this
struggle for power. He already glimpsed the participatory
society in which a man could be Black or White and live
with respect.

One other aspect of Black visibility leads directly into a
consideration of the Vietnam tragedy. The Black man's

roots in an African cultural heritage have been much discussed. Afro-Americanism is bringing this dimension more and more into the center of the Black Movement. Here the Black man confronts White America with a rich, ancient cultural and religious heritage which calls into question the narrowness of American culture, style of life and religious tradition. In this sense, the Afro-American movements are authentic. The Black man has never been simply a creature of White America. He has always been more than the victim of White domination. He links America with a Third World, rooting America in an archaic religious past. He brings into America a personal heritage which counterbalances the narrow rationality of the Puritan heritage and he does all of this in his Blackness. All of these riches are available in America only so long as Black otherness is heeded, attended and respected. White America can do nothing about this except listen and learn. Then White and Black America may have a future in a pluralistic world from which America is now estranged. But that will not be a "White" American future. It will be a global future of many peoples and cultures.

We can treat the Vietnam confrontation far more briefly because the conflict in Southeast Asia has been so thoroughly discussed and the lessons are obvious to almost everyone. Our reflection on this conflict is not intended to resolve political or military issues which have become almost unbelievably complex as the struggle has continued. We are exploring the cultural meaning of the technological society as it has confronted the uncontrollable realities of its world. One of those realities is the Vietnamese determination to survive as an independent culture. With the support of North Vietnam, the Viet Cong in the South has maintained a struggle for independence against the United States on an intense level since 1964. The

United States of America has dropped a greater tonnage of explosives on this small force in a little country than it used in the entire course of World War II. Using the most advanced technology of war, short only of nuclear weapons and obliteration bombing of the North, the United States was fought to a standstill if not actual defeat by the Viet Cong. In its way, this is a remarkable historical event. It may well mark a turning point in military strategies in the emerging global community. Unquestionably it has been a difficult and painful experience for the American people. It drove from the White House a president who had been elected only a few years earlier with a record-breaking majority. What are we to make of this as a challenge to the will-to-domination of the techno-culture?

America's military venture in Southeast Asia can be understood in the context of the policy of containment of communism which emerged after World War II, of which John Dulles was perhaps the most consistent exponent, and of which America's unwillingness to sign the Geneva accords of the Vietnamese struggle for independence in 1954 was part. The accords called for free elections which would have meant endorsement of Ho Chi Minh's regime. Dulles' policy of dividing the world into pro-American and pro-Communist blocs meant that Vietnam's cultural and political independence was suppressed as a significant issue. The only question was whether they were pro-American. A similar policy has been pursued in Latin America, the Middle East and Africa. The United States of America defined itself as free, democratic, peace-loving, the defender of democracy throughout the world. Communism was perceived as a monolithic force which opposed liberty, human rights and a peaceful world. Cultural particularity, nationalism and independent development were thus overridden by America's determination to divide the world along the lines of the Cold War.

This is not to say that Soviet Russia had no designs on world power or that it pursued a policy of pluralistic cultural development. America's perception of a Communist drive for control was not a pure illusion, though it tended to be simple-minded.

Here we would lift up only one of many factors which led America into the abyss of an Asian land-war. The United States of America has carried on a one-way communication in the world, defining and evaluating every situation in American terms and by American standards of productivity. But a global community is emerging which can be a community only if it allows for the genius of particular cultures and religious faiths. Neither Communist hegemony nor American free enterprise can organize a global community. This is a matter of truth and reality, and from this principle a variety of military and political strategies may emerge. But the principle is far from clear to America's politicians and people. We never did and do not now understand Vietnam's culture, traditions, political heritage and possibilities. We have no right on any principle to adjudicate that future. Our support of Diem against the free elections proposed in the 1954 accords was an unwarranted intervention for which we paid bitterly in American lives and resources. But the tragedy of such intervention is that it begets further acts of violence. And so America has moved in recent decades from one tragic impasse to another.

Corollary to the recognition of cultural and religious pluralism, including the right of peoples to develop in their own style of political and economic life, is the recognition of the limits of violence as a political strategy. This reality is, of course, most dramatically evident to America in the threat of nuclear holocaust. However, the transcendence of this nuclear challenge is suppressed by the notion of a balance of terror, so the Nixon administration can win support for escalation of missile defense in the Anti-Ballistic Missile Defense System merely by spreading rumors of Soviet missile strength and the transcendent judgment on violence and domination which should be penetrating American consciousness is suppressed. The Vietnam experience brought America's tradition of domination up short. Cultural and political pluralism had to be faced because America had no serious alternative. We would have suppressed Vietnam in order to maintain our definition of the global situation, but the suppression did not work. So the principle of domination and control which is intrinsic to the techno-culture has come under challenge on a global level. Though it may be suppressed temporarily, cultural particularity is not controllable. America will live in a pluralistic world because it has no choice. Control by the techno-culture is far more limited than we dreamed when we embarked on the "arrogance of power." Soviet Russia is struggling with the same reality as it seeks to control its satellites.

Many other examples of world confrontation could be adduced in support of this transcendent challenge to the American system. One has only to recollect Cuba and even mainland China after World War II in order to grasp the limits of technological domination. So the Vietnamese conflict may yet prove to be the only war America really won. It may illumine and direct a fundamental reconsideration of the principle of economic exploitation which has ruled our global policy. The recovery of the democratic heritage depends upon this external, global challenge. It is no accident that in recent decades America became the symbol of global militarism. The principle of domination has gained ascendancy, and as it has become the governing principle of American life it has produced a global strategy of containment and violence. This is not a matter of wicked leaders but of fundamentally unsound cultural principles. The Vietnam tragedy is an inevitable consequence of such principles. Sooner or later America would demonstrate abroad what it had developed within as a basic principle of life—exploitation of everything by a controlling will which had lost respect for nature, man and God.

Thus we bring to our reconsideration of the democratic and religious heritages the internal and external challenges from Black visibility and the Vietnam defeat. We noted the social and cultural pluralism which Black visibility introduces into American life—high school students may be allowed to wear the Afro-American *dashiki*. Domestic pluralism now finds its counterpart in global pluralism. And if it is taken seriously, the Afro-American strand within America's life forges a link to that global pluralism. Furthermore, we noted the reach toward a human community beyond domination and violence, particularly in the prophetic vision and ministry of Martin Luther King, Jr. We have not begun to absorb his vision, yet we see its confirmation in the Vietnam experience. Domination has not and will not bring global justice or peace. We are now caught in a vicious circle of escalating weaponry. Every resort to arms is justified by fears of aggression and restraint of imperialist ambitions of other powers. Yet each new escalation in arms brings us closer to holocaust and further from justice and peace. We cannot simply abandon our arms, nor can we proceed upon the principle of individual national interest which has dictated our policies since World War II. We need new priorities, new principles to guide us in finding a way through the maze of obligations which accrue to us in an interdependent world. We need a new ordering of values in which productivity and growth can find a limited, secondary place. We need, then, a recovery of transcendence through the challenges which beset us from without and within, so that our civil and religious heritages may furnish us some direction.

RECOVERY OF CIVIL AND RELIGIOUS TRUTH

WE HAVE MADE much of the principle of technological will as the source of America's degradation. This is not a simple and outright rejection of technology. There is virtue in man's drive to be an active agent in his world. The values of the productive culture of the West are obvious to anyone; indeed, technology as a logic of rational control has shown impressive power to sustain life on a massive scale. After all, this new logic makes history less strange and more manageable. But the technological will becomes demonic when it takes on a life of its own in an autonomous system. Then all things become subject to its domination, and a single style of existence suppresses other human possibilities.

The struggle for freedom is essentially the attempt to wrest from the technological order its autonomous power. The challenges to this order reflect the deepening contradictions created by the system. If these contradictions were not present, there would be no dynamic in the world to liberate man from this omnicompetent power. The humanization of technological society depends upon a creative use of these contradictions in the task of liberation. This means enlisting in a cultural revolution to convert the technological order from a principle of exploitative growth to a new principle of humanity. Moreover, that new principle has to be present in the contradictions as the creative movement of this whole system; otherwise an alien principle is introduced and the revolution will lack creative power of renewal.

The new principle for humanizing technology, at least so far as one can discern it from the challenges which we have explored, is that of participation. We give a broad, cosmic meaning to participation when we identify it as the creative principle of a new humanization. We recognized it in Chapter I as the principle of the new global consciousness and the form of man's new sense of membership and dignity. We explored its implications for decision-making in the struggle to have a voice. And we identified it as the central theme in the "religious" movements and rock music of the new generation. So far as one can discern in this transitional period between cultures, participation is emerging as the creative principle for the conversion of the oppressive society to a liberated humanity. One way to explicate this possibility is to interpret our civil and religious heritages in the light of this new principle.

We grasp the creative power of participation by seeing its transformative effects on basic symbols in America's revolutionary heritage: the rights to life, liberty and pursuit of happiness. In appealing to these rights, we make no claim to an authoritative interpretation either in Thomas Jefferson's original formulation or in later appropriations.

Each of these rights has found embodiment and distortion in the triumph of the technological order. The test for a renewing principle is whether it retains the authentic embodiment of the right while overcoming its distortions. In proposing a shift away from America's unwarranted stress on individual initiative, we are claiming that participation adds positive content to these rights in ways appropriate to high technology conditions. And we have seen in the course of these reflections that individual initiative actually passed over to the technological system, so this individualistic dimension of American rights is more honored in the breach than the observance.

The right to life covered a range of protections against undue interference and outside threats. We are seeing more and more of these assurances of life removed in the name of "law and order" but the basic tradition concerned external intrusions or threats to life. Participation sets the right to life in a fuller and more positive context. Men, women and children are upheld in their right to life by participating in the economic resources, adequate housing, medical care and healthy environment which the responsible use of their community's technology can provide. This bears with it, to be sure, the responsibility for the protection of people from the polluting and destructive effects of particular technological developments— whether in sight, sound, atmosphere or eco-conditions. But the fuller meaning of participation is a broader, equalized, inclusive sharing in the resources and capacities of the total society. In view of the global interdependence which technology has created, it is obvious that many of these conditions will have to be provided through global authorities. The monopoly of resources in the hands of selected nations is as outmoded as the telegraph.

In an unpublished paper, "The Breaking of Forms in the Interest of Importance, and Other Iconoclastic Reflections," Bernard Meland spoke of "the broadened base of our humanity" as this had emerged in recent decades. He was referring to the enlarged humanity that came upon our horizon in this post-colonial period. Peoples of Africa, Asia, Latin America and remote islands now share in the forum of world opinion and constitute a richer, more diverse world than any we had ever imagined. And this enlarged humanity is drawn ever more closely together in a material network of interdependence. This is the humanity that sets the boundaries for the imperative of full participation in the right to life and that sets the context for planning population levels and levels of growth appropriate to our life support systems.

Two approaches have characterized planning for the environment: one approach hopes to adjust man and the environment to continued growth and modification; the other visualizes controls and limitations on adaptation in accord with limits posed by the eco-system. Man has constantly been changing his environment since he became a food-producer, so these problems are new only in scale. But here scale makes all the difference, and a participatory understanding of man's nature and being opts for the second alternative—understanding man as participant in a total order of life which he can modify but in response to which he has to set responsible limitations and conditions. Furthermore, man participates in a global, enlarged humanity as well as the natural system of life, so his claims for himself are conditioned by the needs and rights of all men to a healthy life. We recognized this problem in curbing atmospheric tests of nuclear devices, but the destructive effects of some of our industrial developments may be far more damaging to all life on the earth.

Man is not an isolated, individual consciousness who asserts his life over against others, though he often acts this way and in the last century even incorporated such private interests in the oppressive system of a technological order which projected its ambitions over the globe. Man is a natural, communal being who belongs to the enlarged nature which we have discovered in nuclear biology and the enlarged humanity which has rebelled against Western exploitation in recent decades. When the right to life is understood within this participatory reality of man's being, exploitation of man and nature can be understood as the pathologies they really are, and guidelines can be found for global as well as domestic controls. Even though political negotiations and arrangements of most exquisite difficulty remain to be worked out in such a new age, the problems are pressing desperately on peoples everywhere and we need a participatory consciousness which can recognize the very presence of the problems. Consciousness does not solve political problems: but false consciousness can suppress reality, and authentic consciousness can open the way to new levels of political and institutional resolution.

The right to liberty has been crucial in American experience, quite understandably in view of the revolutionary context of the establishment of these rights. Here again liberty was defined to a considerable degree in terms of removal of outside constraints so that men could voice their opinions and share in political processes without undue interference. However, the communal aspects of the rights to life and liberty were played down, ending in a system of protection for private property and large scale enterprises. Staughton Lynd has reviewed this struggle and noted the one-sided character of the emphasis on individual rights to property which emerged from the revolutionary period. His *Intellectual Origins of American Radicalism* points up the presence from the first of a participatory dimension in these rights which was gradually suppressed or neglected. We have already considered the importance of the media in enhancing participation in political processes. We have also examined the importance of sharing in the resources of the community if one is to participate in its cultural and political life. Thus technology is now setting the conditions under which the communal or participatory dimensions of liberty take a precedence which may not have been appropriate under the simpler conditions of '76.

We proposed at the outset that fundamental values in the democratic heritage would find new expression in the unity of a participatory society. Thus far we have stressed the corporate or communal dimension of life for which technology set the conditions though not the institutions. Now we have to assert with equal boldness the principle of particularity or uniqueness of every being which is complementary to any adequate grasp of the concept participation. A person, group or people may not be an isolated consciousness of culture, but each is a particular being which has been formed by a language and a tradition. We participate in a community from a particular place and perspective, out of a particular history and with our own story. America's tradition of liberty, even when it played down the communal dimension in what we might now regard as an extreme way, always upheld the value of particular lives and claims on the world. Now that individual right is being obliterated by the oppressive society. The agonized search of the new generation is often a yearning for this particularity and uniqueness which their tradition had promised. At the same time the recovery of the right to liberty through the participatory society will only lead more deeply into oppression if the particularity of every being is submerged in a collective consciousness.

The implications of particularity for our new age are profoundly significant. Particularity of beings and cultures means that we are talking about pluralism in styles of life, peoples and cultures. The flattening, homogenizing force of the technological order is not participatory, but oppressive. Even the universal standards which come to prevail under conditions of high technology will have to be developed within pluralistic styles of life. This is the import of the right to liberty in a participatory society, and it places even greater weight on the right to a voice in matters affecting one's interests. The federalist polity always understood this need for a voice, though under earlier conditions the crucial need for central planning could be scanted. The basic principle of a participatory society would be centralized, global planning only for necessary conditions to maintain survival of the species in a healthy state, including the ban on destructive agents and limitations on growth appropriate to life support systems.

Our sectarian heritage more than any other kept pluralism before the American consciousness. The sects defended particularity against communal and governmental pressure for uniformity. This is the aspiration of many post-colonial peoples in a rapidly technologizing world. They seek the enrichment rather than the obliteration of their cultural traditions. And despite the tensions between the universal standards of technological systems which will set the conditions of survival and the uniqueness of many cultural groups, technological order can become a means rather than an end of existence if participation in an enlarged humanity considered as particular cultures can set the guidelines for technological innovations and developments.

We have already overlapped aspects of the pursuit of happiness, which has been a less political but more substantive right in the American experience. Pluralism of styles of life and opportunities is an essential aspect of the present struggle for a right to pursuit of happiness. The technological system has extended vocational opportunities, but always within the narrow style of the rationalistic, productive culture. This narrowing of styles of existence is nowhere more oppressively evident than in American schooling, and higher education is simply the magnification of schooling to an nth degree in the name of scholarship and the professional career. We have developed "education" within the technological framework to the point where it is primarily counter-education.

If we take seriously the right to pursuit of happiness, then those who enjoy the productive style of life should be encouraged and rewarded for their activities; at the same time, contemplative, artistic, communal and many other styles of life should be nurtured and supported. Such pluralism is not possible when a universal principle of exploitative growth determines membership in the society and any possible future for persons or groups. This is the source of the oppressiveness of the beneficent system of technology.

Our civil heritage presupposed that certain rights were self-evident. It made appeal to a sovereign deity whose righteousness covered all men, so that those rights were assured in "the Laws of Nature and Nature's God." That ultimate order which formed the backdrop of the civil heritage is seriously in question today, if not by the everyday citizen, at least by those who try to square the world of thought with its major symbols and traditions. We would hazard here the proposal that the crisis of religious meanings in recent centuries, and it is indeed no new issue, has developed out of the obliteration of man's participation in nature and the world through the gradual autonomy of science and technology as an encompassing and universally determinative structure.

America has been nurtured by two faith communities— a community of natural right and a community of biblical faith, the faith community finding expression in Jewish, Protestant and Catholic forms. The civil religion of rights and the confessional faiths were relatively independent but interwoven in the common destiny of a free people. Both communities were ultimately grounded in trust in deity. In the American experience, civil and confessional heritages have furnished renewing transcendence one for the other in different historical periods. We now seem to be at a stage where the confessional heritage is a last hope for renewal and liberation; but this requires a retrieval of the religious heritage.

There are two aspects to the recovery of the religious heritage of the West. The fundamental task is theological: the bondage of faith to man's exploitative domination of the world has to be transcended. The meaning of existence as participation in a pluralistic world, already discernible in the negations of the technological order, has to be explored in the metaphysics which controlled

Western religious development. This is a task to which Paul Tillich devoted his life and in which he made considerable progress. In addition, there is the problem of institutional transformation on which many of us have concentrated attention over the last decades. These two theological tasks are separable but necessarily interrelated.

We argued that racism in America was interwoven with the struggle to realize the obedient will of the Puritan heritage against the contradiction of slavery. This was understood to be a degradation of the Puritan heritage, but its final transmutation has been into the exploitative will of the infallible technological system. But the Puritan heritage itself grew out of an earlier struggle against an objectification of deity in a vision which had come into the possession of a religious institution. Thus the control of deity in religious institutions was overcome only to surrender nature, man and God to control by a human institution—the technological order. Where the good was once understood as that which the holy institution prescribed, we now enjoy that liberty and good which the productive system permits. This is the encompassing meaning of goodness for our world.

The religious crisis of the West arises from the struggle to overcome the hegemony of this new deity of technology. In rejecting that deity, we are fighting for man's participation in nature and history against his historic entanglement in centuries of global imperialism and his resistance to any otherness which constrains his greed and lust. This demonic force of technology is not alien to Western religious development but rather intrinsic to the absoluteness of Western claims for its religious truth; it triumphed in a final desperate attempt to found religious absoluteness in a human, obedient will. Once that fragile human will was replaced by the omnicompetent and omnipotent will of the technological order, reality became that which the system projected and truth disappeared. Projections of the system, then, constitute the reality of other peoples and cultures, justifying their subjugation and raising encomiums for those who exploit them.

Participation and pluralism point us beyond the unreality of technological projects, directing us toward the truth of man's belonging to history in finite, limited and particular ways. It rests on a fundamental trust that history is for man, though our last century of blood baths would seem to contradict this faith. Participation means recognition of the full participation of deity in this historical enterprise. To recognize holiness and grace in human history is to take the finitude of deity and man's enterprise seriously and to turn with new respect to particular peoples, cultures and faith traditions. It thus relativizes the Christian claims which have been such a demonic force in the world. And it opens the Western world to participation in global experience which had been closed off by its own pretentious wisdom.

The task before religious institutions is similarly difficult and revolutionary. Religious leaders have been troubled by the isolation of religious life from public matters for a long time. In various theological reflections (including my *New Creation as Metropolis*), many of us put considerable weight on the organization of power in the public sphere as the avenue of renewal of the religious heritage. It now seems evident that this was an inadequate analysis. The participation of religious life in the public sphere is crucial in a cultural revolution, but the central issue is not organization of power but disclosure of meaning. This is a more radical but more viable situation for religious institutions, because the struggle between exploitation and participation pervades every facet of American life. This struggle has no specific location. It is the universal struggle for renewal of life in the West and on global terms, and it can be pursued wherever and whenever men and women will reflect on a fundamental level about their own despair and the human possibilities of our world. Political involvements would then become even more controversial, but each mode of participation in the cultural revolution would seek to develop a new consciousness and commitment to change.

Renewal of religious institutions has been plagued with the dichotomy between pastoral and prophetic ministries, cult and common life. As the shape of the cultural revolution emerges, the unity of the religious task is now evident in an agenda of liberation and a common participatory style. The problem with much previous discussion of religious renewal has been the attempt to settle the unity of ministry in political, or ideological terms, but this approach merely repeated in religious form the hegemony of the exploitative will as the meaning of human existence. Thus, the technological system dominated the modes of theological as well as sociological analysis. The participatory consciousness makes the private sphere far more political in a fundamental sense, since it draws out the conspiracy in exploitation which American privatization now shares. On the other hand, participation also challenges the political partisans who end up vying for control of the system which consumes the world and threatens life itself. Liberation to an enlarged humanity and the relativity of Western religious experience can set an agenda of truth in which private and public come into question and man's hopes gain a hearing.

"Unwilling Journey"

Recovery of our civil and confessional heritages is essential to sanity and truth in a world whose reality is only the next stage of technological expansion. For America as spearhead of this global exploitation, this means an era of agonizing self-criticism and revolutionary struggle. In the words of Helmut Gollwitzer's title for his account of his experience as Russian prisoner of war, America is entering upon an "Unwilling Journey." Gollwitzer used this phrase to refer to his journey through a Soviet labor camp as a member of the German Wehrmacht. He had enjoyed the privileges of the German uniform during the victories of the German army. Like many others he wished to shed the uniform when the Soviet victory was imminent. Like many others he was taken upon that "Unwilling Journey" of purgation. Gollwitzer is, of course, pointing to the divine will under which that journey was made, and grace abounds in his searching account. The title fits our American situation well. We have enjoyed the comforts and privileges of the techno-culture. We have lived by the fruits of domination. Now we are facing the demand for reparations. We have lived by nuclear terror, and now we are threatened with terror. We have lived through enslavement and imperialism, and now we face the reproach and guilt of our past. Now we enter upon this "Unwilling Journey" not seeing a way ahead, only hoping for a renewal of life and promise in what we shall confront. The possibilities are there, opening before us in challenges of transcendence. The question is whether in grace we can find liberation to open ourselves to judgment and promise, whether this "Unwilling Journey" can become a way to freedom in an enlarged humanity.

The Black Manifesto— Abridged*

To the White Christian Churches and the Synagogues in the United States of America and to All Other Racist Institutions:

Introduction: Total Control as the Only Solution to the Economic Problems of Black People

Brothers and Sisters:

We have come from all over the country burning with

* Robert S. Lecky and H. Elliott Wright, eds., *Black Manifesto: Religion, Racism and Reparations* (New York: Sheed & Ward, 1969); for full text see pp. 114–126.

anger and despair not only with the miserable economic
plight of our people but fully aware that the racism on
which the Western World was built dominates our lives.
There can be no separation of the problems of racism
from the problems of our economic, political, and cultural degradation. To any black man, this is clear.

But there are still some of our people who are clinging
to the rhetoric of the Negro, and we must separate ourselves from these Negroes who go around the country
promoting all types of schemes for black capitalism.

Ironically, some of the most militant Black Nationalists,
as they call themselves, have been the first to jump on the
bandwagon of black capitalism. They are pimps; black
power pimps and fraudulent leaders; and the people must
be educated to understand that any black man or Negro
who is advocating a perpetuation of capitalism inside the
United States is in fact seeking not only his ultimate destruction and death but is contributing to the continuous
exploitation of black people all around the World. For it
is the power of the United States Government, this racist,
imperialist government, that is choking the life of all
people around the world.

● ● ●

Racism in the United States is so pervasive in the men-
tality of whites that only an armed, well-disciplined,
black-controlled government can insure the stamping out
of racism in this country. And that is why we plead with
black people not to be talking about a few crumbs, a few
thousand dollars for this cooperative, or a thousand dollars which splits black people into fighting over the dollar.
That is the intention of the government. We say . . . think
in terms of total control of the United States. Prepare
ourselves to seize state power. Do not hedge, for time is
short, and all around the world the forces of liberation

are directing their attacks against the United States. It is a powerful country, but that power is not greater than that of black people. We work the chief industries in this country, and we could cripple the economy while the brothers fought guerilla warfare in the streets. This will take some long-range planning, but whether it happens in a thousand years is of no consequence. It cannot happen unless we start. How then is all of this related to this conference?

• • •

BLACK MANIFESTO

We the black people assembled in Detroit, Michigan, for the National Black Economy Development Conference are fully aware that we have been forced to come together because racist white America has exploited our resources, our minds, our bodies, our labor. For centuries we have been forced to live as colonized people inside the United States, victimized by the most vicious, racist system in the world. We have helped to build the most industrialized country in the world.

We are therefore demanding of the white Christian churches and Jewish synagogues, which are part and parcel of the system of capitalism, that they begin to pay reparations to black people in this country. We are demanding $500,000,000 from the Christian white churches and the Jewish synagogues. This total comes to fifteen dollars per nigger. This is a low estimate, for we maintain there are probably more than 30,000,000 black people in this country. Fifteen dollars a nigger is not a large sum of money, and we know that the churches and synagogues have a tremendous wealth and its membership, white America, has profited and still exploits black people. We are also not unaware that the exploitation of colored peoples around the world is aided and abetted by the white Christian churches and synagogues. This demand for $500,000,000 is not an idle resolution or empty words. Fifteen dollars for every black brother and sister in the United States is only a beginning of the reparations due us as people who have been exploited and degraded, brutalized, killed and persecuted. Underneath all of this exploitation, the racism of this country has produced a psychological effect upon us that we are beginning to shake off. We are no longer afraid to demand our full rights as a people in this decadent society.

•   •   •

But to win our demands from the church, which is linked up with the United States Government, we must not forget that it will ultimately be by force and power that we will win.

We are not threatening the churches. We are saying that we know the churches came with the military might of the colonizers and have been sustained by the military might of the colonizers. Hence, if the churches in colonial territories were established by military might, we know deep within our hearts that we must be prepared to use force to get our demands. We are not saying that this is the road we want to take. It is not, but let us be very clear that we are not opposed to force and we are not opposed to violence. We were captured in Africa by violence. We were kept in bondage and political servitude and forced to work as slaves by the military machinery and the Christian Church working hand in hand.

Port Huron Statement: Students for a Democratic Society—Abridged*

We are people of this generation, bred in at least modest comfort, housed now in universities, looking uncomfortably to the world we inherit.

•   •   •

* Paul Jacobs and Saul Landau, eds., *The New Radicals: A Report with Documents* (New York: Vintage Books, 1966); for full text see pp. 149–162.

Our work is guided by the sense that we may be the last generation in the experiment with living. But we are a minority—the vast majority of our people regard the temporary equilibriums of our society and world as eternally functional parts. In this is perhaps the outstanding paradox: we ourselves are imbued with urgency, yet the message of our society is that there is no viable alternative to the present. Beneath the reassuring tones of the politicians, beneath the common opinion that America will "muddle through," beneath the stagnation of those who have closed their minds to the future, is the pervading feeling that there simply are no alternatives, that our times have witnessed the exhaustion not only of Utopias, but of any new departures as well.

• • •

The search for truly democratic alternatives to the present, and a commitment to social experimentation with them, is a worthy and fulfilling human enterprise, one which moves us and, we hope, others today. On such a basis do we offer this document of our convictions and analysis: as an effort in understanding and changing the conditions of humanity in the late twentieth century, an effort rooted in the ancient, still unfulfilled conception of man attaining determining influence over his circumstances of life.

• • •

We regard *men* as infinitely precious and possessed of unfulfilled capacities for reason, freedom, and love. In affirming these principles we are aware of countering perhaps the dominant conceptions of man in the twentieth century: that he is a thing to be manipulated, and that he is inherently incapable of directing his own affairs. We oppose the depersonalization that reduces human beings to the status of things—if anything, the brutalities of the twentieth century teach that means and ends are intimately related, that vague appeals to "posterity" cannot justify the mutilations of the present. We oppose, too, the doctrine of human incompetence because it rests essentially on the modern fact that men have been "competently" manipulated into incompetence—we see little reason why men cannot meet with increasing skill the complexities and responsibilities of their situation, if society is organized not for minority, but for majority, participation in decision-making.

* * *

We would replace power rooted in possession, privilege, or circumstance by power and uniqueness rooted in love, reflectiveness, reason, and creativity. As a *social system* we seek the establishment of a democracy of individual participation, governed by two central aims: that the individual share in those social decisions determining the quality and direction of hs life; that society be organized to encourage independence in men and provide the media for their common participation.

In a participatory democracy, the political life would be based in several root principles:

that decision-making of basic social consequence be carried on by public groupings;

that politics be seen positively, as the art of collectively creating an acceptable pattern of social relations;

that politics has the function of bringing people out of isolation and into community, thus being a necessary though not sufficient, means of finding meaning in personal life;

that the political order should serve to clarify problems

in a way instrumental to their solution; it should provide outlets for the expression of personal grievance and aspiration; opposing views should be organized so as to illuminate choices and facilitate the attainment of goals; channels should be commonly available to relate men to knowledge and to power so that private problems—from bad recreational facilities to personal alienation—are formulated as general issues.

Bibliography

Baldwin, James. *The Fire Next Time.* New York: Dial Press, 1963.

Boulding, Kenneth E. "The Economics of the Coming Spaceship Earth." In his *Beyond Economics: Essays on Society, Religion, and Ethics,* pp. 275–87. Ann Arbor: University of Michigan Press, 1968.

Brown, Claude. *Manchild in the Promised Land.* New York: Macmillan Co., 1965.

Carmichael, Stokely, and Hamilton, Charles V. *Black Power: The Politics of Liberation in America.* New York: Vintage Books, 1967.

Conant, James Bryant. *Slums and Suburbs: A Commentary on Schools in Metropolitan Areas.* New York: McGraw-Hill Book Co., 1961.

(Cox Commission Report) *Crisis at Columbia: Report of the Fact-Finding Commission Appointed to Investigate the Disturbance at Columbia University in April and May 1968.* New York: Vintage Books, 1968.

Ellison, Ralph. *Invisible Man.* New York: Random House, 1952.

Ehrlich, Paul. "Eco-Catastrophe!" *Ramparts*, September 1969, pp. 24–28.

(Eisenhower Commission Report) Graham, Hugh Davis, and Gow, Ted Robert. *The History of Violence in America: A Report to the National Commission on the Causes and Prevention of Violence.* New York: Bantam Books, 1969.

Fanon, Frantz. *The Wretched of the Earth.* New York: Grove Press, 1963.

Flacks, Richard. "The Liberated Generation: An Exploration of the Roots of Student Protest." *Journal of Social Issues* 23 (September 1967): 52ff.

Fry, John R. *Fire and Blackstone.* New York: J. B. Lippincott Co., 1969.

Gollwitzer, Helmut. *Unwilling Journey: A Diary from Russia.* Translated by E. M. Delacour. Philadelphia: Muhlenberg Press, 1953.

Grodzins, Morton. *The Metropolitan Area as a Racial Problem.* Pittsburgh: University of Pittsburgh Press, 1958.

Handlin, Oscar. *Race and Nationality in American Life.* Garden City, N.Y.: Doubleday & Co., Anchor Books, 1957.
———. *The Uprooted.* New York: Grosset & Dunlap, 1951.

Harrington, Michael. *The Other America: Poverty in the United States.* New York: Macmillan Co., 1962.

Herberg, Will. *Protestant, Catholic, Jew: An Essay in American Religious Sociology.* Garden City, N.Y.: Doubleday & Co., 1955.

Jackson, Merrill. Keynote Address, National Advisory Conference on Generating Manpower for Mission, Chicago, Illinois, Oct. 10–12, 1966.

Keniston, Kenneth. "Social Change and Youth in America." In *Youth: Change and Challenge*, edited by Erik H. Erikson, pp. 161–87. New York: Basic Books, 1963.
———. *Young Radicals.* New York: Harcourt, Brace & World, 1968.

(Kerner Report) *Report of the National Advisory Commission on Civil Disorders.* New York: Bantam Books, 1968.

Kozol, Jonathan. *Death at an Early Age: The Destruction of the Hearts and Minds of Negro Children in the Boston Public Schools.* Boston: Houghton Mifflin Co., 1967.

Lecky, Robert S., and Wright, H. Elliott, eds. *Black Manifesto: Religion, Racism and Reparations.* New York: Sheed & Ward, 1969.

Long, Charles. "The Black Reality: Toward a Theology of Freedom," *Criterion*, Divinity School, University of Chicago, Spring 1969.

Loubser, Jan. "Calvinism, Equality and Inclusion: The Case of Afrikaner Calvinism." In *The Protestant Ethic and Modernization: A Comparative View*, edited by S. N. Eisenstadt, pp. 367–83. New York: Basic Books, 1968.

Lowi, Theodore J. *The End of Liberalism: Ideology, Policy, and the Crisis of Public Authority.* New York: W. W. Norton, 1969.

Lynd, Staughton. *Intellectual Origins of American Radicalism.* New York: Pantheon Books, 1968. See especially Chapter 3: "The Earth Belongs to the Living."

Malcolm X, with the assistance of Alex Haley. *The Autobiography of Malcolm X.* New York: Grove Press, 1966. See especially p. 185.

Marcuse, Herbert. *An Essay on Liberation.* Boston: Beacon Press, 1969.

———. *Eros and Civilization: A Philosophical Inquiry into Freud.* New York: Vintage Books, 1955.

———. *One-Dimensional Man.* Boston: Beacon Press, 1969.

McDermott, John. "Technology: The Opiate of the Intellectuals." *New York Review of Books*, August 31, 1969.

McLuhan, H. Marshall. *Understanding Media: The Extensions of Man.* New York: McGraw-Hill Book Co., 1964.

McLuhan, H. Marshall and Fiore, Quentin. *The Medium is the Massage.* New York: Bantam Books, 1967.

Meland, Bernard. "The Breaking of Forms in the Interests of Importance, and other Iconoclastic Reflections." Paper read to the faculty, Divinity School, University of Chicago, October 1969.

Oglesby, Carl and Shaull, Richard. *Containment and Change.* New York: Macmillan Co., 1967.

Pitcher, Alvin. "Race and Civil Disobedience: Two Cities— Two Churches." *CTS Register* vol. 57, no. 6 (May, 1967): 1–6.

Roszak, Theodore, *The Making of a Counter Culture.* Garden City, N.Y.: Doubleday & Co., Anchor Books, 1969.

Schultz, William C. *Joy: Expanding Human Awareness.* New York: Grove Press, 1967.

Servan-Schreiber, Jean Jacques, *The American Challenge.* Translated by Ronald Steel. New York: Atheneum, 1968.

Smith, Lillian. *Killers of the Dream*. Garden City, N.Y.: Doubleday & Co., Anchor Books, 1963.

Solzhenitsyn, Aleksandr I. *One Day in the Life of Ivan Denisovich*. New York: Praeger, 1963.

———. *The Cancer Ward*. New York: Dial Press, 1968.

———. *The First Circle*. New York: Harper & Row, 1968.

Terry, Robert. *For Whites Only*. Grand Rapids: W. B. Eerdmans Publishing Co., 1970.

Theobald, Robert. "The Background to the Guaranteed-Income Concept." In *The Guaranteed Income: Next Step in Economic Evolution?*, edited by Robert Theobald, pp. 83–96 and Appendix. Garden City, N.Y.: Doubleday & Co., 1966.

Tillich, Paul. *Systematic Theology*, vol. 1. Chicago: University of Chicago Press, 1951.

Van Hoffman, Nicholas. *We Are the People Our Parents Warned Us Against*. Chicago: Quadrangle Books, 1968.

Wade, Richard C. "Urbanization." In *The Comparative Approach to American History*, edited by C. Vann Woodward, pp. 187–205. New York: Basic Books, 1968.

(Walker Report) *Rights in Conflict: A Report Submitted by Daniel Walker, Director of the Chicago Study Team, to the National Commission on the Causes and Prevention of Violence*. New York: Bantam Books, 1968.

Wright, Richard. *Native Son*. New York: Grosset & Dunlap, 1940.

———. *White Man, Listen!* Garden City, N.Y.: Doubleday & Co., 1957.

Recommended Readings

The struggle for freedom in high technology societies is creating a whole literature of technical advice and social criticism. Since the present volume represents a single perspective on this complex field, it may be useful to suggest some readings to broaden the comprehension of the interested reader. Since the cultural revolution is a movement rather than a school of thought, the most interesting readings are appearing here and there in journals of literary and social criticism. One thinks of the work of figures such as Paul Goodman, Ivan Illich, John McDermott, Jerome Bruner and many others. If we slight these important contributions in the following recommendations, it is only in order to isolate a few introductory readings which can broaden the background of concerned readers.

THE CULTURE OF TECHNOLOGY

Boulding, Kenneth E. *The Meaning of the Twentieth Century: The Great Transition.* New York: Harper & Row, Colophon Books, 1965.

Ellul, Jacques. *The Technological Society.* Translated from the French by John Wilkinson. New York: Vintage Books, 1964.

Ferkiss, Victor C. *Technological Man: The Myth and the Reality.* New York: George Braziller, 1969.

Fromm, Erich. *Toward a Humanized Technology.* New York: Bantam Books, 1968.

Marcuse, Herbert. *One-Dimensional Man: Studies in the Ideology of Advanced Industrial Society.* Boston: Beacon Press, 1964.

ORGANIZATION OF HIGH TECHNOLOGY SOCIETY

Birnbaum, Norman. *The Crisis of Industrial Society.* New York: Oxford University Press. 1969.

Galbraith, John K. *The New Industrial State*. New York: Signet Books, 1968.

Harrington, Michael. *The Accidental Century*. Baltimore: Penguin Books, 1965.

Myrdal, Gunnar. *Challenge to Affluence*. New York: Pantheon Books, 1962, 1963.

SCIENCE, TECHNOLOGY AND ENVIRONMENT

Commoner, Barry. *Science and Survival*. New York: Viking Press, 1963, 1964, 1966.

Dubos, Rene. *So Human an Animal*. New York: Charles Scribner's Sons, 1968.

Ehrlich, Paul R. *The Population Bomb*. New York: Ballantine Books, 1968.

COUNTER CULTURAL MOVEMENTS

Keniston, Kenneth. *Young Radicals: Notes on Committed Youth*. New York: Harcourt, Brace & World, Harvest Books, 1968.

Lasch, Christopher. *The Agony of the American Left*. New York: Vintage Books, 1969.

Yablonsky, Lewis. *The Hippie Trip*. New York: Western Publishing Co., Pegasus, 1968.

The notable omission in this list of topics is the racial crisis and the new literature of the Black Intellectuals and social critics. The literature is already too extensive and diverse to allow for selections that would do more than indicate the present author's interests. The present volume ranges over many aspects of the racial crisis, and several relevant and important works are listed in the Bibliography.